WRITINGS 2

Contributing Writers

Tatay Jobo Elizes

WRITINGS 2

Contributing Writers

1 - There Is Hope For The Philippines - Grace Padaca
2 - Pointers On Employment Abroad - Melanie Aquino
3 - Without KNCHS: (Love story) - Toto Causing
4 - 422 Years Ago - Rodel Rodis
5 - Filipino American History Month - Rodel Rodis
6 - A Need For Reflection - Gloom - Cesar Torres
7 - Did Ninoy Die For Nothing - Joey Concepcion
8 - Criteria - American Institute of Philanthropy
9 - Coming Revolution In The Ballot - Cesar Lumba
10 - 2009 - A Retrospective - Cesar Lumba
11 - Strangers In Our Own Country - Casiano Mayor
12 - The Gypsy Soul - Casiano Mayor Jr.
13 - An End To Cheating - Sonny Coloma
14 - Toward Culture of Giving - Sonny Coloma
15 - Reasons to be Proud Pinoys (satire) - Anonymous

Barcode Area

We will add the barcode for you.

Made with Cover Creator

Tatay Jobo Elizes

Self-Publisher

Tatay Jobo Elizes was born in Manila, Philippines, in 1934, now retiree, based in NY, busy writing and self-publishing as a hobby and involved in piglets dispersal programs for livelihood projects in the Philippines via the internet. **Gratitude and acknowledgment** belong to those who contributed their writings and those who encouraged me to continue publishing these writings book series. **I dedicate this book** to the **Filipino people**, and affectionately to my wife, **Cora**, my children, **Tetchie, Chevy & Abeth, and Marie & Bimbo,** my grandchildren, **Karines & Aung, Noelle, Chad, Marjo, Jeb, Marvin & Marty,** great-grandson **Jason Win** and my siblings **Susan, Hilda, Bobby, Bey & Manny** and to all my extended relatives and friends alike.

ISBN-13-978: 1477676790   **ISBN-10: 1477676791**

Content

Introduction

Writings are mirrors of the times and history. Let me explain why I publish writings. **You don't have to be a good writer** to write something. The only requirement is to write in simple terms to be understood. I have seen a lot of good writings in the internet, in magazines and newspapers. But most writers have only one or two articles and therefore not enough material to be published as a book. And yet, many of them need to be published. So the idea of collecting all these various writings hibt me. I myself cannot come up with enough material. I decided to offer my services to publish anybody's worthwhile writings in one fairly good sized book, in paperback or pocketbook form. Their ability to publish is solved in a nutshell.

I am offering these services free of charge because of the availability of print-books-on-demand (POD) system nowadays. I have acquired the knowledge the hard way. I am now in a position to help publish writings of anybody. I can produce the book, but it's not entirely free of cost on my part. I merely assume the cost.

Why put your writings in a book? And not just in the internet? I recommend that writings be retained in a hard copy or in book form or printed form for posterity. The book will always be there among your collections or libraries. Not all use the internet. The internet access has its technical problems. Writings in the internet may be erased erroneously. Free storage is hard to access. Paid storage may be returned or lost. CDs, DVDs, memory cards, and other forms of electronic storage need players.

For those looking for a publisher, especially if you have a novel or many essays, I can produce the paperback book under your own authorship. Book sale is risky business. In most cases, I cannot even recover my initial costs. As authors, you must help in marketing these books that contain your writings.

1 – There is Hope for the Philippines

Former Gov. Grace Padaca
Province of Isabela

Gov. Padaca *was born in 1963, an accomplished CPA, finished BSBA-Accounting, magna cum laude at Lyceum, 2-time elected Isabela govenor, was famous radio host of Bombo Radio DZNC for many yeas in Isabela, received numerous awards and commendations as civic and political leader and practicioner, both locally and in USA. Has proven record of leadership and outstanding achievement despite her handicap as a "lady in crutches due to polio."*

(Speech Delivered at Philippine Military Academy Alumni Assoiation, Inc (PMAAAI) Convention at General Headquarters, Armed Forces of he Philippines, Camp Crame. Wednesday, 1 April, 2009, 2:29 PM)

Good Morning, everyone. Thank you so much for the honor of speaking before you today.

I know how special PMA'ers are. When I was still a radio broadcaster, I interviewed a lot of you, from the AFP, the PNP, the AIRFORCE, from Lieutenants to Generals, from Scout Rangers to rebel soldiers. I covered the visits to the 5th ID in Camp UPI, Gamu, Isabela, of many Chiefs of Staff and Army Chiefs.

I conceptualized and hosted a program called Hindi Trabaho Ito, Personalan Lang (This Is Not Work, This is Persobnal), that featured the other side of government officials, military and civilian, para malaman din ng mga listeners namin ang personal side ng mga opisyal (to enable the listeners know the personal side of the officers and officials), so that their more humane and soft side are discovered.

I once sang on the air with General Angelo Reyes when I interviewed him while he was the 5th ID Chief in Upi, Gamu, Isabela. Ang kinanta namin (We sang) "Paint My Love" by the group Michael Learns To Rock.

I covered a lot of turn-over ceremonies of Generals retiring from the service to at last, "Do Apostolic Work, as I remember General Rey Alcasid saying, "Apostolic Work" means "Mag-alaga ng Apo (Baby-sit grandchildren)." The latest retirement or turn-over ceremony I witnessed was that of General Melchor Dilodilo about two weeks ago before he was replaced by General Ochoa in the 5th ID.

The difference now is I witness such events and command conferences no longer as a media person but as Governor of the largest province in their AOR.

Perhaps many of those who were assigned to Cagayan Valley and the Cordilleras from the mid-80s until the year 2000 who I interviewed as Bombo Grace never had the inkling that the physically handicapped radio broadcaser would one day replace the very powerful men of the Dy dynasty in Isabela.
I never had any inklng either. My visions or dreams did not

reach that far. As someone who grew up with polio since the age of three, I consciously limited my dreams to what I thought I could at least achieve and there were not many of them, and certainly not being Governor of one of the largest prvovinces in the country. If I had a dream it was simply to be a good radio announcer because it was a job where I could be heard but not seen. I was very shy, you see, as a result of my physical handicap.

In the year 2001, I did shock the people of Isabela when I dared run for elections. Yes, tumakbo ako sa elekyon kahit hindi ako makalakad (Yes, I ran for election despite the fact that I could hardly walk.) And worse, I was running to fight the one family that ruled our province for more than 40 years.

I come from an ordinary Filipino family. My parents were both public school teachers who taught us, their six children, to live simply so that we could make both ends meet.

I finished school and became a Certified Public Accountant (CPA) but the Lord has a way of granting our deepest wishes. My first major job was yes, as a broadcaster in the local radio station in our province, Bombo Radio Cauayan, so I became a Cerified Public Announcer instead.

For fourteen years I was a Broadcast Journalist, anchoring a radio program called "Sa Totoo Lang," (For the truth only), that went on the air for three hours every single day, news and issues came through me - giving me often a close-up view of the abusive way by which resources of our government were being squandered while our poor people kept getting poorer by the day.

The political DYNASTY (of the Dy Family) in Isabela began its rule in our province as early as the year 1963, from the father, to the sons and he had many sons because well, he had many wives. That was public knowledge. They did not make any effort to hide it from the public. I feared the example they were giving to our young people and even the government officials under them. Aside from the father and the sons were the generation of the even more numerous grandsons automatically waiting next in line. Padami sila nang padami (Their dynasty continues to grow) . Parang gremlins (Just like gremlins). They have become so used to being in power that many times, they did not care anymore about what the people thought or felt. They forgot that power is not theirs as a birthright. It is the people's.

You who have been assigned to Isabela or the 5th ID who came in with the PMA values, specially integrity, also must have felt disgusted with how power was being used in Isabela. That is, not to serve the people but to enrich and emower themselves and their cronies.

I told myself, I cannot just sit here looking at these things happening. This is not what I have been taught democracy should be. Hence, the elections in the year 2001, I filed my candidacy against Faustino Bojie Dy III for whose sake every effort was made so that he would run unopposed.

Grace Padaca

My chances of winning were almost nil but I said, at least, even if I lose, I would have peace of mind. I will not be one of those complaining why evil things were being done to us as a people, feeling mad and frustrated, but not lifting a finger anyway to stop them.

As a candidate, I was taunted. They said I was crazy. The powerful men of the dynasty laughed me off. They did not take me seriously, well, until it was time to count the votes.

This woman who could not walk, ran! for the elections and trounced the machos in Isabela.
And Grace lived happily ever after? Of course not! It turned out

winning the elections was the easiest part. Governing is a totally different story. Humanda si Obama! (Prepare Obama!)

The first three years of my being Governor were very difficult. If they cannot kill your body, everyday they will try to kill your spirit. . . I had to live with all the blows from everywhere that came my way, from all the Dy-nasty's people in the capitol that I was surrounded with.

I inherited almost A Billion Pesos in debt when I took over as Governor, mostly for projects contracted just before the elections of 2004. One after the other we were able to pay them.

I am now in the middle of preparing my state of the province address. The last time I delivered one in January of 2007, I reported to our Apo Isabelinos that for every three pesos of the capitol's obligations to contractors and suppliers, we have by then already paid two or almost 70%. When I report to them again in a couple of weeks, I will update them that our obligations to our suppliers is down to 15%. We could have paid it all, if not for the many irregularities in the transactions that's keeping me from paying.

We were able to settle these obligations, while at the same time not failing in paying the 700 Million Peso Loans borrowed from the banks by my predecessors. We have so far paid 400 Million Pesos of the Principal and 200 Million Pesos of the interests. Imagine paying almost 50% interest. In my administraton, we no longer contracted any new loans from the banks.

Still, we were able to enrol 100,000 of our indigent Isabelinos to the Philhealth Program without them having to pay a single cent.

The change in leadership in Isabela also resulted to many big changes that we all have been longing for as a people.

One is the upliftment of the living conditions of our farmers which make up more than 60% of our population. With our one million heactare land area, we are the country's second largest province next to Palawan. We are the biggest corn producers in the entire Philippines and the second biggest palay producer, next to Nueva Ecija. In order for our farmers to enjoy better prices for their corn and palay produce, we are using provincial governmet funds// to add up to P3 per kilo// of their harvests. We do this through our partnership with the National Food Authority. I remember that when I was still a broadcaster, just a difference of 25 centavos or 50 centavos in the price per kilo of rice and corn was already a major thing with our farmers. Now, we are giving them subsidy of three pesos per kilo. We can even go as high as five pesos if we find it necessary. Because of this, we are able to influence upwards the trend of prices in the market simply because we give our farmers an option that they did not have all the past years of the Dy-nasty in Isabela. For this price subsidy program, we won a Gawad Galing Pook Award last year.

Unlike my opponents, when I campaigned I did not demand from the rice traders and other businessmen money for the elections, that is why when I won, I had not the burden of being indebted to them and also that's why I can freely do what is needed for our poor farmers. I always hasten to emphasize this though I am not against businessmen. During the campaign, I told them as long as you do things fair and aquare, I will let you be. Makakatipid kayo sa akin dahil hindi ko kayo huhuthutan. Wala kayong kailanang bawiin sa mga magsasaka dahil wala akong hihingin sa inyo na para bang mayroon akong ipinatago. (You can save your own money because I will no extort from you. You need not exploit the farmers because of this as I dont owe you anythng.)

I have always told our people that after freeing ourselves from the 40-year dynasty that lorded over us that the battle is not yet over. We may have defeated the dynasty but there are other things that we have to continue to fight. We also have to free ourselves from our own wrong attitudes, from our misplaced values, our bad habits. That we should just rely on others to do the thinking for us. I repeat to them over and over again, mas masarap tulungan ang mga taong marunong tumulong sa kanilang sarili. (It's sweeter to help those peole who know how to help themselves.)That they should not only expect to receive help, 100%, they should also do their share in making their lives better for the future. I tell them, use me as your visual aid. It is easy to see that with my physical condition, I also need a lot of help but I have no used this as an excuse to be just a burden to others.

With the power and resources that I have in my hands, we were able to re-focus the priority of the provincial government to the truly most needy of barangays, regardless of the number of potential voters living there or whether or not the Mayor is an ally of the Governor. We have instituted an Ugnayang Bayan or Our People's Day every Wednesday when people from the barangays can directly talk with me. After only one year of implementation, about 90% of the province's 1018 barangays received financial assistance for projects directly from my office, without the barangay captains needing to go through the mayors. I always remind barangay officials that if they do not do well in their joint projects with me or do any hanky-panky, I will ignore them and turn to NGOs or People's Organizations in their barangays who will be my partners in giving services to their constituents. That becomes deterrent enough.

I also had my experience of being persecuted or wanted to be recalled by most of the mayors of Isabela but eventually when they saw that I was effectively cooperating with more and more barangay officials, they started to cooperate, too. Even some of the most rebid supporters of the old admnistration started testing the waters.

When I came in, only one or two of the 36 Mayors of the province of Isabela were supportive of me. But after four years, the situation is reversed. I am friendly enough with most of them that I have invited 33 of the 36 Mayors to the presentation ceremonies of the Ramon Magsaysay Awards last August. And they came. Yung iba nga nagpa-autograph pa sa akin. (The others even asked for my autograph.)

For the past four years of my being Governor, it has been clearly proven that it is not true that I am an NPA member, a charge hurled against me by my opponents in their desparate attempt to find a reason why this person, who they dismissed as nuisance, defeated them. When they tried to block my proclamation in 2004 by charging me of terrorizing voters through the NPAs, it was the military officials who volunteered to execute affidavits in my favor, specially General Orly Soriano, General Homer Capulong of the 102nd Brigade, and my friend, the late Captain Jose Rene Jarque. They knew how I did my job with objectivity and fairness.

Even if some people became quite curious about the NPA branding of me, I did not allow it to limit my actions. I continued reaching out to everyone, specially those in the remotest barangays, the so-called NPA areas. Aren't they the ones who feel most neglected by the government hence they go up the mountains and take up arms? Now when they come to the capitol, we attend to their concerns promptly so that they don't find the need to take to the streets or mountains anymore. The people in govenmcent are listening to them and attending to them. Lagi kong sinasabi sa kanila, sana makabawas man lamang ako sa mga dahilan ng inyong paghihimagsik. (I always reminded them that hopefully my presence in government is able to reduce their dissidence.)

Let me share with you one very special moment in my life as Governor. This is about an NPA Commander and a Brigade Commander who I always interviewed when I was still a broadcaster. Wala pang cellphones noon, mayroon lang mga two-way radio or single side bands whatever, I do not know. (There were no cellphones yet, only 2-way radios and single sideband sets). But I went through the great pains just to be able to bring the two men to dialogue in my radio programs before. Sabay silang naririnig. (They can be heard simultaneously.). That was made possible because I like to think they had some kind of a mutual respect for each other. Perhaps in the way they conducted themselves in battle or maybe even in the fact that they were willing to talk to each other. In 1992 the NPA Commander surrendered to then Governor Benjamin Dy and who took him in and is now a capitol employee. His name is Rolando Lee or Ka Ilyan. The Brigade Commander was General Homer Capulong. Colonel pa lang siya noon (He was a Colonel.) Hanggang ngayon text mates pa rin kami. (Until now we are still text-mates.) Last year, he came to Isabela to invite me as graduation speaker in the Wesleyan University of Nueva Ecija where he is one of the Board of Trustees. I asked him, "General, gusto mo bang makita ng personal si Ka Ilyan" (General, do you want to see Ka Ilyan in person?) So here they were. This was one of the nicest moments of my life as a broadcaster and Governor.

Another step that I initiated is to meet with the poor men's lawyers, the PAO's (Public Attorneys Office), to learn from them their predicaments and those of their indigent clients. Even before the enactment of RA 9406 last March 2007 which authorizes local government units to give financial and other support to our PAO's, I already worked for the inclusion of allowanes for the Public Attorneys in Isabela's annual budget and from then on they have been receiving regular allowances and assistance from the Provincial Government. With regard to judges, prosecutors and clerks of court, I have emphasized that I have agreed to continue what the previous leaders of Isabela were giving them for their allowances but only as augmentation to the insufficient amount that they are receiving from the national government, not to solicit assurance that they will spare my people if they ever get into trouble. As a matter of fact, as in the case of PDEA'cs Major Marcelino, I have some issues too with prosecutors in Isabela who let people go scot free even if they are already caught red-handed.

FOREST PROTECTION

Right now, in Isabela, I am in the middle of a very difficult mission that I decided to take head on. This is the fight against the big syndicates in Isabela who have been rampantly destroying the Sierra Madre mountains which is located in 9 out of 36 municipalities. It is in Isabela where 30% to $0% of the country's remaining forest cover remains.

So many times a day, for too long now, trucks full of illegally cut logs pass through our highways undeterred by the DENR, while we lose millions of Pesos in crop and infractructure damages when typhoons and floods hit us due to denuded forests.

Natural disasters hit us so many times a year. It it's not the waters, it is the lack of them that cause untold suffering to our farmers and poor families, like when the drought in 2007 damaged the equivalent of our whole provincial budget for the year.

I worked with our Sangguniang Panglalawigan (Provincial Board) and they approved my request of appropriating P8 Million of our own money in order to help put a stop to the unabated cutting of trees in our part of the Sierra Madres.   Of the one millon board feet waiting to be brought down from the Sierra Madres which have already been cut by people called bogadors, we have confiscated about 60% or 600,000 board feet. We are set to auction this off and DENR Secretary Lito Atienza agreed to our request that we use the proceeds to continue suporting the Isabela Protection Task Force. It's no joke providing for the meals of our Task Force members morning noon and night as well as those of platoon of soldiers, who are helpng us a lot in this anti-illegal logging fight.

This reminds me of the time of retired General Orlando Soriano as Commanding General of the 5th ID when his task force Luntian and the DENR's Oplan Jericho confiscated trucks upon trucks of illegally cut logs in Isabela. I remember na galit na galit sa kanya noon ang Dy-nasty. (I remember that the Dynasty was very angry at the General).

Last September, in coopration with the 45th IB and the CASF assigned in Isabela, we flew over the Sierra Madres and proved my worst fears. The one million board feet of illegally cut logs that we have blocked in the town of Ilagan is nothing compared to the estimated ten million board feet that we saw in the town of San Mariano, still a part of the Sierra Madre natural park.

Ten million board feet, only for this year 2008?

How about all these past years? How can I not take an active role in this fight to protect our forests?
There are so many things in Philippine society hat we have to fight: corruption, politics of patronage, jueteng, illegal logging, etc.

Many times I have talked with Mayors in Isabela about the issues and they'd always tell me, "Governor, we have no choice, because so many poor people come to us for their urgent needs." These mayors use people's poverty as a convenient excuse to receive bribe or protection money. Many often refuse to do the courageous thing because they are afraid they will lose their sources of funds and the votes for the next elections.

I have seen many government oficials stop short at doing the right thing. They look the other way. No matter how strong their feelings are about what should be . . . they do not act. They are immobilized by their fear of losing votes. Sabi ko tuloy (I concluded) that such obsession with re-election is even more paralyzing than polio.

Sabi ko sa kanila, kayo naman pala ang pilay. Hindi ako. Dahil ganito lang ako, kumikilos ako laban sa illegal logging, sa jueteng, sa gumagawa ng hindi tama. (I told them, you are not lame. I am lame due to polio. But despte this handicap, I fight illegal logging, the numbers gambling, and all forms of anomalies.)

I refuse to waste the power that my position gives me not to do what only Governors or Government executives like me have the opportunity or the power to do.

Let me tell you one of my biggest realizations as Governor.

After having been in this position for four years, I have confirmed for myself that truly, people in government positions have enormous powers. One signature of mine can cause the release of millions of pesos. One yes or no that I say affects he lives of so many people. If used well, power can be a good thing. It can make you do so many things to uplift the conditions of many poor people. It can make you give strength to the weak. It can make you empower the common man.

But if you are not grounded, if you have not the right values, you can easily get tempted. Lalong naging malinaw sa akin na nakakatakot mapunta ang kapangyarihan ng pamahalaan sa kamay ng mga hindi karapatdapat. (It's become clearer to me that it's very fearful if government power should go into wrong hands.)

I am well aware of disappointments among many PMA'ers who very well know what should be but do not see it in society, more so in government.

Mukhang pagod na rin ang mga tao sa people power (People are tired of people power) as we know it and of course coup d'etat is not acceptable to many.

But we should not stop feeling disgusted with what's happening. We shoculd unite and decide what to do with our anger, with our frustration. As I have said, we will not have peace of mind if we just allow wrong to prevail in our dear country without lifting a finger to help change things.

For one, let us not put all our hopes and expectations on one person alone. Our country's issues cannot be solved by asking just one person to resign or reform. We will only be frustrated. Let us instead work for the election into office of good governors, good mayors and even good barangay captains and kagawads so that if we are not satisied with the people at the top, there are still the local governments to rely on.

That is what our group, Kaya Natin (We Can Do It), is advocating. Kami po nina Among Governor Eddie Panlilio of Pampanga, Mayor Jesse Robredo of Naga City, Governor Teddy Baguilat of Ifugao, Mayor Sonia Lorenzo of San Isidro, Nueva Ecija and Harvey Keh of the Ateneo School of Government. Kaya Natin (We Can Do I) is a movement for good governance and ethical leadership.

We have been going around, specially in schools trying to engage the young and explaining to them the need of registering to vote, being well-informed of issues, and more importantly, making themselves available and ready when volunteers are needed to ensure better elections in the country.

I am quite obsessive on the matter of electoral reforms.

Because ever since my re-election as Govrnor last year and seeing once again how the electoral process has become even worse, I would tell anyone who would care to listen that we should not wait until just three months before the elections to cram and do our voter's education, to encourage volunteers and not just leave the pollwatching to a handful of sacrificing CWL or Legion Of Mary members or mothers-volunteers and let elections be dominated by the well paid machinery of traditional politicians.

Sadly, sometimes, it is also during election seasons when police and military officials are relieved and reassigned in a way that government neophytes like us can only look in hopelessness and shock.

Fortunately, there are now groups like the MGG or Movement for Good Government composed of different organizations which as early as now are working for better elections in 2010. It is good that they are non-partisan, that they are involving themselves not for benefit of any candidate but the over-all orderly and credible conduct of the coming elections.

Yesteray, Cito Beltran wrote about a PMA Alumni Association Chapter in Malacanang, saying that the Palace has been overrun by retired military and police officials who are all graduates of the PMA. I do no know the reasons of the President for making this so but personally, I do not mind graduates from the PMA joining the government, perhaps not by sheer apointment but victory through elections. Sayang na po ang galing ninyo, at ang bababata niyo pa naman kung nagre-retire. Mas may kaya naman kayo sa iba. Naturuan naman kayo todo-todo sa Academy tungkol sa courage, integrity, loyalty, not to mention excellence in the things that you do. (I'ts a waste of talent for you to retire early. You are young and more talented than others. You have been taught in the Academy courage, integrity, loyalty, not to mention excellence in the things that you do.) I take exception though on those who, despite being PMA'ers, did not or are not doing anything to fight jueteng. Sometimes, the more junior officers seriously want to act but those in the higher positions are the ones thwarting their efforts. I hope it's not true what I hear about the wait till you become a syndrome. If not jueteng, it is taking protection money from illegal loggers or drug lords. What a waste of great power of our dear soldiers and policemen if these are used to perpetuate rather than stop the evils of society. The dirty money from jueteng, drugs and illegal logging, all these years, have been putting so many of the wrong and unworthy people in what I consider as sacred positions in government.

Let us please change the situation. I know that you from the PMA can do so much towards this end. Whenever I talk to our people about political dynasties, I tell them hindi lamang dito sa Isabela mayroong dynasty. Marami din naman sa ibang lalawigan. Pero at least, sa iba, pinag-aaral muna nila mga anak, inagdadalubhasa, pinapaaral ng abogasya or public administraion kasi alam nilang sila ang papalit. Dito sa Isabela, sabi ko, yung mga myembro ng pamilya hindi nag-aral kasi mananalo lang din sila. Nagpapakasawa munang maging bum, pag ayaw na makaisisp maging mayor, congressman at nanalo. A least man lang sana, paghandaan naman nila ang maglingkod sa tao at sa bansa. (Dynasties exist also in other provinces, not only Isabela. At least in other provinces, they send their children to schools of higher learning to prepare them for political office, but not in Isabela, where children are encouraged to become bums, without any knowledge of good governance, due primarily to their wrong perception and self-assured posture that public offfice are theirs by right.)

What I am trying to say is that PMA'ers have been taught so much about love of country and its people and many of you have experienced relating with the poorest of our poor in our remotest barangays. That can be put to good use, well, if not in direct means as thru elective positions in government then in many other areas where you can continue using the knowledge, wisdom and experiences that you as PMA'ers have been uniquely provided.

If somebody so disadvantaged like me can make it despite the fact that I do not have the money, political machinery and sophistiation with electoral cheating that traditional candidates have, it means there is still hope in the Philippines, that Filipinos can look beyond what is wrong and usual, as long as we guide them, educate them, make them see the difference. We have to build on this hope and not let it slip from our hands.

If I have to say so myself plase look at me, this handicaped person who is now the Governor of my people. Look at me as the embodiment of the power of the people through the ballot. What else can explain my being governor than the decision of the Isabelinos to use their right to vote differently. Mine was only one vote. What made me win was the vote of hundreds of thousand of others. They who made the choice and because of this, they have a different Isabela now. Let us then work for the wise use of the people to vote and protect and respect their choices.

Lastly, please realize that the very few among us who are said to give our people hope, also need to be encouraged, also need to be uplifted.

We canot fail. Please help us not fail. When I delivered my response during the Ramon Magsaysay Awards presentation ceremonies, I mentioned about Barack Obama talking about his Audacity of Hope, but many of us Asians, who have suffered so much more, and have already succeeded in rising above our many challenges, need now to talk about the burden of the brave - the need to continue succeeding after raising the hopes of our people. Because if we ourselves fall short of expectations, the lower still that we have sunk the faith of our people. But the good news is I know well enough that so many of our fellow Filipinos support those who fight for what is right.

I know it from all the encouragement and cheers that I get when I meet ordinary Filipinos - salesladies in department stores, security guards, waiters and waitresses, as well as professionals, business executives and even among our soldiers and policemen. As long as our kababayans still feel offended and disgusted with the wrong things happening in our country and at the same time clamor for change, we will have a better Philippines.

Let me end my sharing with you today by relating to you one incident in year 2001, when I first dared run against the powers-that-be Dy in Isabela.

There was a candidates' forum called by the Comelec and the PPCRV NAMFREL where we candidates were asked our platforms of government. We were given only 5 minutes each.

Sabi ko sa sarili ko, naku, paano yan, sa bagal kong maglakad, baka ubos na iyong 5 minutes ko pagdating ko sa podium. (I told myself, poor me, with my slow steps, I might not even reach the podium in 5 minutes.)

When I shared this story to one of those who attendd he candidates forum, he said, you did not even have to talk, Grace.

You, yourself, were the message.

That here is someone who people perceive as someone weak, someone helpless, but still cares enough for her country to help make it change.

That is till my message. I have been given so many opportunities to share my thoughts about nation building. And my message continues to be. Nobody is exempted from the duty of doing our share so that we Filipinos can start taking control of our own future and working together for that genuine and lasting change that we all want to see in our country. How much more if you are a PMA'er? I know. You know that. I know too - that many of you - want to do that. But by this time, we should know what works, and what does not. What will last, and what will not.

Thank you for allowing me to share with you my humble experience. Please remember that if little me can do something, our big PMA'ers, you can do a lot more or our country - but only in the right way - and for the right reasons.

Maraming salamat po. (Thank you very much.)

Gov. Grace Padaca, Province of Isabela

2 - Pointers On Employment Abroad

Melanie Aquino

Taken from her famous blog, PINOY NEWS. She's an orthodontist @ 23, a traveler at 35, a wife @ 38, a mother @ 39 and a dreamer, working at making things better.....always

Dateline, Tuesday, November 03, 2009

How I found work in Saudi Arabia

My surprise departure for the kingdom I wrote in a previous blog I applied at yahoojobs and posted my resume. My target country was the U.S. then and I knew back then that I would ONLY be hired as a dental assistant or hygienist even with my credentials as a dentist. I never did expect that a recruiter in Saudi Arabia was looking for an orthodontist.

A local recruitment agency called me one day, asking me if I wanted to go and work in Saudi Arabia. Huh? Never in my mind was there a thought to consider the middle east. But I kept an open mind. The first things I did, in chronological order (each step discussed thoroughly on the next blogs):

1. I told my father and mother about it, and my significant other.

2. I Checked out poea.gov.ph to see if the recruitment agency was licensed, meaning not suspended or license revoked or cancelled.

3. Since the recruitment agency could not answer any of my "million" questions, they directed me to my employer who was kind enough to correspond by email, skype, gtalk or he would call by phone.

4. He sent me a contract which I immediately showed to a lawyer friend of mine to comment on. Then correspondence between my employer and me continued until we were both satisfied.

5. Make the decision to whether take the offer or not.

6. If you decide on taking it, proceed to "recruitment" procedures. Start by renewing your passport if needed.

Wednesday, November 04, 2009
1. Telling My Family I have an Offer to Work in Saudi Arabia
This was my first time ever to leave the country for work. Moreover, the first time to leave for a country so different from ours....the home of the Islam faith. I actually had no idea what I was getting into. I viewed it as exciting, an opportunity that may never pass again. So even before telling anyone, I had to educate myself as to what I was getting into.

These are the better information available now:
http://www.escapeartist.com/efam/56/Working_in_Saudi_Arabia.
html
http://a-pinoy-in-nz.blogspot.com/2006/09/factsmyths-about-life-in-saudi-arabia.html
http://americanbedu.com/2008/03/06/a-womans-life-in-saudi-arabia/
http://taraummomar.blogspot.com/2009/03/susies-new-life-in-

saudi-arabia.html

Lastly, I think the most important reference guide to working in the kingdom is to be up to date with: http://alexasuncion.multiply.com/ especially now that the Saudi Labor law has been translated in English AND FILIPINO.

Start asking yourself what questions your family would be asking you and be prepared to answer. For me, the 1st and hardest question asked was WHY SAUDI ARABIA?

My answers:
1. I was working for the past 6 years as an orthodontist and I was not progressing as fast as I wanted to.
2. I wanted to have savings...yes, during that time I just opened a clinic and was on a 0 savings level.
3. There was no other offer where I could work at the level I was in...an orthodontist....not having to downgrade into a dental assistant or hygienist.
4. I wanted an adventure, a time for myself, a period of independence, of earning my keep, being responsible for myself.

Then followed a series of questions which I called the easy questions....where will you live, salary, when are you going home, Are there Pinoys in your workplace, etc...I took down all their questions because these were the same questions I would ask my employer.

If you are in a relationship, not yet married or married, I must say it is truly very hard being apart. You must really think doubly hard whether you need to be separated for 2-3 years. Look at all options and considerations as:

1. Who will take care of the children? Can the one staying in the Philippines afford to stay home with the children?

2. Is there a chance for you to be together. Actually there is, if the profession you are getting into has "FAMILY STATUS". By

this I mean that you will establish residency and then have your family follow you after 3-5 months. Most doctors and professionals (bankers, engineers) are hired with "family status" .

3. If this is the only option that one of you has to leave, be sure to keep an open communication with the family. Prepare an internet connection on the computer. Buy a webcam and teach the whole household how to SKYPE, do GTALK and how to email.

Tuesday, November 10, 2009
2. Check out the Philippine Overseas Employment Agency (POEA) website
The POEA website is very helpful in:

1.Verifying the legitimacy of your Philippine based recruitment agency

Found this under **OFW ADVISORY**:

Beware of recruitment agencies with cancelled or suspended licenses

The POEA advises the public to be wary of recruitment agencies with cancelled or suspended licenses that are still actively recruiting for overseas jobs.

The POEA, as of September 14, 2009, has cancelled the licenses of 454 recruitment agencies since the start of its operations and placed 44 others under preventive suspension. For 2008 and the first eight months of 2009 alone, the POEA cancelled 76 licenses and suspended or fined 57 agencies as a result of recruitment violations.

Please click HERE to verify status of recruitment agencies.

2. Articles for / about Overseas Foreign Workers

3. Articles for / about Foreign Employers

4. Articles for / about Recruitment Agencies

5. Articles of memorandum of Agreements between the Philippines and other countries

6. Overseas Employment Regulations
7. Vacancies

8. .They even have an e-registration for the pooling of Manpower where you submit your resume and they store it for possible interest of foreign employers.

Tuesday, November 10, 2009
3. Correspond with your Employer
This is a series detailling the steps on how I dealt with a Job Offer from SAUDI ARABIA. I feel it would also apply on any job offers anywhere in the world.

Important steps discussed previously was (click the link for reference):
1. Tell your family and important people around you and educate yourself about the country you intend to work in.
2. Check out the POEA website.

The 3rd is to Correspond with your employer.
The recruitment agency would facilitate contacting the employer for you. Just say you would like a personal correspondence with the employer. Ask that he call you, or (for lesser cost) chat / talk through yahoo messenger, google gtalk or skype.

This way:

a. You can directly ask your "1 million" questions. Best to store the conversation if it is a chat or if talk, try to write down important details you can look back to, just in case you need further clarifications later on.

b. You will personally hear the sincerity of your employer and viceversa. He will be able to find out, even interview you already and viceversa.

In this conversation be ready to ask and be asked.

My questions basically were:
1. Who is my employer?

You will be having a Saudi sponsor in your stay. You will be under his responsibility and he will pay for all your expenses: airfare, VISA. Your VISA will be in your passport.

Be sure your occupation is accurately written on your VISA.

My experience on this was my entry VISA had me written as a nurse for my occupation. This was told to me early on (best be informed) by my employer because he only had NURSE VISAS then. But still I was able to work as an orthodontist, was also able to take the Professional Licensure exam. Not really sure if my employer had to "pull some strings" so still best to have all information accurate and correct.

2. What is my work specifically? (job description)

This will also be written down on your contract

3. How much is my salary?   (yes don't be shy to ask).

4. Where is the company / facility located?

This will help you gauge how far you are from the Philippine embassy (one is in Riyadh, the other in Jeddah). I felt fairly secure working within Riyadh, the capital city. Google map the exact location.

5. Are there Filipinos in your company?   If it would not be a bother, ask permission to contact a Pinoy employee and have a

conversation with him about ....everything.

6. When do you expect to arrive in the work place? This is important to know because October to March are very cold months in the kingdom. Best to be ready with the right clothes for the cold season.

7. May I know my accomodation?   Home accomodations are usually provided for by the employer. Either it is near the company/facility or maybe even within the compound / building.

8. Practices I should know within the country and the workplace?

This was 1 question I forgot to ask, but here are some MUST KNOWS:

a. On arrival at the airport, your passport will be taken from you (this will be the last time you will see your passport until you need it again in your next vacation / flight home)
b. On arrival at the airport, be ready to line up and follow all the instructions. click for more info.

b. All men and women are always segregated. Men go out only with men unless with married couples.

c. A man and a woman is discouraged to talk alone. Talk always in a group.

d. If you are of a different religion other then ISLAM, do not bring religious relics, novena, bible (all of your faith you may see in the internet)

e. Women should always be accompanied by a male guardian (husband, company guardian/driver) when going out All the rest of their culture you can find out at the PDOS (Pre-Departure Overseas Seminar) you will be attending soon before you leave.

9. When is my vacation? For how long and who pays for my airfare and back?

Filipinos usually go home during the Christmas holidays (booking is soooo hard). Say your preference or some employers already tell you that you can only spend vacations during non-peak months of business. You must know this so you will be amenable to having vacations during summer months (Saudis usually spend vacations abroad from August to September) or if you wish on christmas, kindly request your employer for early booking to be sure to get home.

I remember my first vacation, I got home just in the nick of time, afternoon of December 25. I forgot to ask my employer to book early. By early I mean even a year before your vacation or 6 months before you intended vacation, at the latest.

Vacations are usually once a year for 1 month, all expenses paid by the employer. But some request twice a year for 2 weeks each. This depends on your employer.

10. Will I get my full salary on my vacation?

All vacations / one month must be paid. You will get this upon your return to the kingdom.

I hope anyone reading this, who has more recent info and would want to help by sharing will do so by writing a comment below :-)

Monday, November 16, 2009
4. What is important to see in Your Saudi Employment Contract
This is a series detailling the steps on how I dealt with a Job Offer from SAUDI ARABIA. I feel it would also apply on any job offers anywhere in the world.

Important steps discussed previously was (click the link for reference):

1. Tell your family and important people around you and educate yourself about the country you intend to work in.
2. Check out the POEA website.

3. How to Correspond with your employer

The 4th Consideration is scrutinizing your job/work contract.

I was sent a contract via email. Employee/Worker Contracts in Saudi Arabia are written both in English and Arabic. I immediately sent it to

a. a Filipino lawyer-friend who commented on the contract to make sure all areas covered.
b. a friend presently residing in Riyadh who could verify things for me.

CONTENTS OF YOUR JOB CONTRACT
(Should be written on Company Stationery with company seal and address):

1. Date that the employment contract is executed between the 1st & 2nd party
2. First party / employer. This is the Company's name and name of your Saudi National Sponsor
3. Address, Tel No., Mobile No. of employer / Company
4. Representative agent / Agency / Recruitment Company and its address in the Philippines and abroad
5. Second Party / employee. Nationality. Passport #. Date/Place of issue. Permanent address. Contact Numbers.
6. Terms and Conditions:
a. Position. Job description. Workplaces (This is important so you may know in advance where in the kingdom will you be possibly assigned because your company may have other branches or sister companies). Best for you to research about the place & Pinoys in the area.
b. No. of years of effectivity of contract (usually 2 Gregorian years. Note that there is a different Islamic / Hijri calendar)

Always request Gregorian calendar usage.

c. Salary / month in SAR (SAUDI RIYALS). End of Service Benefits (ESB). If your salary is supplemented by percentage income, commissions, be sure it is written down.

d. Additional Benefits:

1. Accomodation. Is either provided for or you are given an allowance to rent for a year. If accomodation is provided, list down contents of the accomodation. Usually this is decided upon by employer, as to which to give.

2. 30 days Paid Leave which includes airfare. Time is decided either by employee or employer depending on what suits the business.

3. Trial Period of 3 months. If after 3 months, the employer finds you not suitable for work, he may terminate contract and with/without compensation. Be sure you are compensated during the 1st 3 months and is written in your contract. If the employee finds it best to terminate contract,employee will shoulder the cost of going back to his country.

4. Other incentives: In addition to salary, there may be percentage income or commissions. Be sure to ask if there are other incentives like this and have it written down.

5. Medical Insurance provison. Very important to ask if you get sick or meet an accident, what are the policies of the company. Up to what extent is their provision or support.

6. Paid sick leave. How many days in a year (usually 10 days) with medical report & acceptable
with administration. If more than 10 days, not ompensated. If more than a month, may be terminated with the employee bearing the cost of transport back to his country.

7.Conditions by which the employer and employee may terminate this contract.

8. Company policies important to note in the contract (company holidays, working hours, engaging in other business within the kingdom while an employee, settlement of disputes). If possible ask for an employee's handbook or Company Rules and Regulations.

9. This must be incorporated in the contract. "That if there is a need to modify or add/delete any item, it shall require the

signature of both the employee and employer.

Sunday, November 22, 2009
5. Making the decision to Take the Overseas Job or NOT
For most it is as easy as considering the financial rewards of an overseas job that prompts the decision to leave or not. For some, just the thought of running away from the heavy burden of staying in the Philippines is the motivating factor.

But I realize now that I have left and come back, just what are the important considerations in leaving for an overseas job?

1. Monthly wage and benefits. The cost of living here and abroad is not the same. Do not be quick in deciding just because your salary was tripled. Consider / ask your employer and research on the following:

a. Food allowance . Find out how much it would cost to feed yourself for a month. Include that in your expenses. Back in 2007, SR200-300/month was enough.

b. Accomodation provision or allowance. One cannot own a property in the kingdom so the sponsir usually provides a room/unit accomodation, alone or shared. Or can give you the freedom to look for your own place (with Filipinos) by giving you a monthly allowance. In 2007, SR1200/month for a 2 bedroom unit.

c. Transportation allowance. A bus or means of transport is usually provided to and from work to your accomodation. Otherwise, ask for it or an allowance.

d. Medical Insurance. Expensive to get sick in the kingdom so be sure you are protected.

Maximize on your additional benefits other than your salary so that you have more to send back home to your family. There is no TAX in the kingdom, by the way.

2. Be sure you are near HELP when help is needed

a. Have Pinoy co-employees and friends help you. While still in the Philippines, establish Pinoy contacts in the kingdom. Find out their contact numbers and converse with them by phone or email or chats.

b. Know how far you are from the Philippine embassy. This is a true story of a lady bus conductor here in the Philippines who was in the news back in 2007 (Arab News) who spent almost 20 years in a very remote town of the kingdom, left all by herself to fend for herself as a domestic helper. Her employer left her alone and she survived by planting and feeding herself on goats which she raised herself. She could not be reached because of the "remoteness" of her area. Oh God!

3. Settle your family and businesses before you leave.

a. If you leave who will take care of your children? How will your spouse handle your leaving? Will he continue to work or stay in the house for the children?

b. Who will handle the finances of the family? Who will receive your remittance?

c. How will your family communicate with you?

d. If you are leaving a business, end it properly. Consider if you do come back, will you have something to come back to?

IN SUMMARY, your final decision to leave or not would depend on what you will get in salary and benefits, how much help you can get from Pinoys in the kingdom and the state of your family and businesses when you leave.

Bottomline is whatever your decision, be sure its is wholly yours and not a decision made by others' opinions of you.
Monday, November 30, 2009

I will take the Job Offer In the Kingdom, What's next?

After following all the blog entries before this, it is time to go and embark on your new adventure.

First go to your recruitment agency and they will ask you go through a medical check up in an accredited hospital. Back in 2005, I spent around P2-3,000 for this. I had a 9- hour fast (stopped eating at 12 midnight and made sure I was in the hospital by 7 am to have a waiting allowance of 2 hours) for my blood tests, and brought with me my

1. Sample feces in a clean small container

2. Urine sample I submitted while waiting for my turn in the hospital the next day I waited for my medical report to come out before proceeding to the next steps below.

Here are the steps I did to prepare for my leaving the Philippines:

1. Prepare my passport. If your passport will expire in a year or 2, best to renew it while in the Philippines. Renewal fees in the kingdom through the embassy is more expensive. Have your passport picture taken, prior to appearance to the DFA. Be sure to wear a coat or any shirt with a collar. Personal appearance is required but you can make an appointment for yourself via the internet. Choose to have a machine-readable passport, although more expensive (P950 than the usual P750), this is what all passports will be eventually. Follow the steps on Passport application or renewal here.
2. Prepare my birth certificate / marriage certificate.
Best to apply for a NSO (National Statistics Office) certified birth certificate. They have serbilis centers you can actually go to or if you can't go, have a representative get it for you with an authorization letter and your ID (SSS, Driver's license or any valid ID). Or if you can't have it done by others or yourself, you can have it delivered. Just follow the steps here.

3. Prepare my school credentials

a. Go to my school registrar and ask for:
1). Transcript of Records (atleast 2 copies or even more), certified true copy (both for undergraduate and post graduate courses)
2). . Ask for a Certificate of Graduation, and / or certified true copy of your Diploma (undergraduate and post graduate courses)

c. On acquiring my transcripts and diplomas, I proceeded to the Commission on Higher education (CHED) where they Certified, Authenticated, and Verified (CAV) all my transcripts and diplomas. Follow the steps here. All other CHED services which you may need, here. CHED sitemap here.

4. Prepare my work experience credentials

a. Asked my superiors for certificate of employment stating my job, position and years / period of service.

b. This will be certified / notarized by the Regional Trial Court (RTC) in the Manila City Hall. I went to any Notary Public at the Manila City Hall and they helped me process these documents. Fee is about p150 per document to be notarized.

5. When School and Work Experience credentials have been certified, I went to Malacanang to have it certified (AGAIN). I did this on commute because there are already public transportation that has a route from Malacanang to the Manila City Hall.

6. After Malacanang certification, go to the Department of Foreign Affairs for "ribboning" or final certification.

7. I made sure I had a xerox copy of all my documents before submitting them to my recruitment agency. They then scheduled me for a PDOS (Pre-Departure Orientation Seminar). This is free.   Important things I learned from the PDOS:
a. Buy the small arabic book on how to speak arabic / learning

arabic (around P150 back in 2005)

b. Get your PDOS certificate and open an account in Metrobank, BDO or BPI where you will open an OFW account and deposit P100 as maintaining balance. Be sure that when you open the account, you have with you a co-depositor here in the Philippines who can have access to your account and receive the remittances you will send (preferably family / relatives). Important to show your PDOS certificate as this will be your passport in opening the account.

c. get yourself an accident / life insurance if you still have extra money.

Going through the 7 steps it would be safe to prepare around P7 - 10,000 for all the fees that have to be paid.

Just a word of advice, plan each trip as early in the day as possible. Each step entails a long line, and a lot of waiting so best to start the day early...leave the house as early as 5:30 or 6 am.

3 - Without KNCHS: I Could Not Have Loved And Cried

Toto Causing

Atty. Bertini "Toto" Causing is the lawyer of the National Press Club, based in Manila. He is one of the most active advocates and exponents of Jury System for adoption in the Justice System in the Philippines.

What do you think you would be today if Koronadal National Comprehensive High School (KNCHS) did not exist from the start?

Imagine KNCHS were not born. You could have studied high school somewhere else. You could have graduated from Notre Dame of Marbel for Boys or Girls or from King's College. Or, you could have not studied at all because your parents were too poor to support your secondary education. Or, if your parents' means could permit you could have gone to other far places.
Imagine KNCHS were not born. In any case, you could have not met your classmates and friends with whom you shared special moments inside its sprawling campus. In other cases, you could have not experienced love for the first time: a love that you can proudly say as "true love" no matter others call it "puppy love" or simply "first love." Some of these resulted in marriage among two alumni.

Nevertheless, in my case, without KNCHS I could have not felt the "true love" I have never had in my life.

I always wanted my true love to be kept in my heart's closet. But it had not occurred in the manner I wanted. From its onset, that secret spilled over to the knowledge of some of my classmates at KNCHS because of my recklessness that let my feelings out through my actions, which we learned then as "louder than words." I cannot forget those laughs that came to me as jeers. But most importantly, without KNCHS I could have not met the girl I loved - and still love today.

I cannot forget the stupidity I did when I gave three roses to the one I loved right after the flag ceremonies one day. I overcame the fright in me although the chill still gripping all over me. In one unguarded moment within that unforgettable moment of my life, one of the stems of the roses broke down, bowing to the overpowering presence of the one I loved. This sent my male classmates into controlled laughs deep inside. I felt so ashamed but I immediately told myself, "What could I do now that it was done and that it cannot be undone anymore?" That was the first and the last time I ever give roses and these went to that girl I love. The breakdown of the stem proved to be an omen that this love would never grow and never would be reciprocated to make it as one beautiful love story.

I cannot also forget the day when I wrote my first--and last--love letter. I could no longer remember the words and the gist of the message I wrote. But I can remember my fear for she might find faults in my writings. I can still clearly see my self buying a pink stationary and write the love message on it. I could not explain why my hands trembled that my hand erred in writing the words. So I had to go back to the bookstore whose name I could not recall to buy three more stationary cards to ensure that if ever I commit mistakes again I would still have spares. At last, I finally overcame the fright and completed what to me a profound message of love. I gave it to the girl I loved -- and still love till today -- but I could no longer remember how I was able to have that card reach her hand.

After letting off that card of love from my hand, I felt an overpowering shame in me. I wanted to get it back but I could no longer do it. I was ashamed that I wanted to hide in our house and never attend classes at KNCHS anymore so as not to be seen by the girl classmates of my beloved. I was fearful of the laughs and smiles that would meet me whenever I would cross path with my beloved or her girl classmates. Nevertheless, the madness of my father seeing me hesitant in going to school compelled me: His Chinese bamboo stick proved to be the one I feared the most.

As soon as I got inside the KNCHS campus, the one I was scared about took place: I met my beloved and her classmates she was usually with every time I would see her. At that very moment, I resigned to fate, waiting for an ax to fall on me. Thanks God, the laughs or smiles never showed up. But I still got so nervous and when I was walking I felt like I was like falling to the ground in extreme shame. Nevertheless, I could not resist my urge to take a look at the eyes of my beloved; so that I shot my look and it happened that her tantalizing eyes met mine, sending me chilling to the bones. At any rate, that made my day and I was so happy. I thought she also loved me and that thought was enough for me to stay a healthy high school student.

I also recalled wanting to know how did my beloved feel about my love letter. I was so ashamed to approach her in school or accompany her in coming home from school or visiting her at home; we were too young to engage in love and her parents might scold me. I know they had a house phone but our house had none. So I decided to look for a phone where I can secretly call her at a time I thought she would be at her house. I found one but I could no longer recall where it happened. That was a big old black phone that rang scandalously that you cannot find today. And when I tried to insert my finger on the dial holes to rotate my hand, I failed to complete the three numbers for my fingers trembled, so that I hanged up the phone. I thought for a while and tried to battle my fear. And when I thought I should call her, I tried to insert my finger again and it chickened out anew that I put back the big black phone piece. I examined my self again and asked me if I should really make that call. Many thoughts again cropped up in my mind. I was thinking, "What if his father would be the one who would pick up the phone, what should I say when he would ask who was this boy wanting to talk to his pretty daughter?" I was also thinking, "What if it was her mother who happened to pick it up?" I did not find any answer to these questions except to say to myself, "Come what may."

Finally, I managed to complete the phone number and I heard the ring from the other end of the line. I was lucky. It was my beloved who happened to answer and I know it because her pretty voice sent love emoting from my heart. I was stammering and I did not know what and how to say. After all, I managed to say what I wanted to say. I asked her if she had read my letter and she said, "Yes." I said to myself, "Oh my God." I continued stammering out words, telling her, "What... do... you... say... about it?" I could not recall now what her exact answer but the gist was this: "Can you wait for ten years?" Oh my, the message sent me some hope that my love for her would be reciprocated and hopelessness that I will have to suffer for a decade because I had to wait for ten long years. Thirty years have passed now, it has yet to happen.

In all the days inside KNCHS in all those years that she was still there, her face filled up my thoughts most of the time. Even inside the classroom, I would daydream of me and her as lovers in a paradise. Every time I had free time from school, I would sit in places where I would wait her pass by and each time I would see her it would never occur that our eyes would not meet each other's. In one of these days, I recall that one Saturday I was driving a bicycle to the public market for an errand; and that when I passed by their house, I turned my head leftward and my eyes were glued at it. I was looking for her for my day would not be complete without seeing her. As I was daydreaming over the bike, my chin suddenly hit hard on something so hard, only to know that I hit the back of the roof of the tricycle I was tailing: I did not know that it stopped to pick up a passenger. I fell to the pavement and got some injuries. But I never felt any single pain and I said to myself that I should not cry or I might be seen by my beloved and I would be embarrassed extremely. So that after I was berated by the tricycle driver for being careless, I immediately asked for forgiveness and assured him I was okay. Oh my, even if blood kept dripping off my injuries, I went straight to the public market to do the errand. The injuries did not leave a scar but that moment has been nailed in my mind forever.

This "love trip" of mine somehow ended when my beloved graduated with honors a year ahead of me. She went to Notre Dame of Marbel College where she graduated again with top honors. When I graduated the next year, I went to Mindanao State University in Marawi City . Even there at the 1,000-hectare campus that is cold like Baguio the whole year round and one that was teeming with beautiful college students, my mind kept coming back to the thought of seeing the face of my beloved. I was set up several times by my college classmates, friends, roommates and fraternity brothers and sisters with several girls but I never had the urge to have a girlfriend there. Thus, until I graduated from MSU, I did not enter into a relationship with any girl. The thought of my first love was so overpowering that I was still nurturing the dream to marry someday the girl of my love that was born inside the campus called "KNCHS."

After coming back to my hometown, I was preoccupied by thoughts of finding work and at the same time take the board examinations for civil engineering. And my plan was that after I find myself stable enough, I would court my dream girl relentlessly and convince her to marry me.

But I went to Iloilo where I found myself working for a community as their community engineer. After a year, I left for Manila to find my luck. In all these years, the thought of my beloved girl was still at the top of my agenda every day. But I was weak to fulfill that dream.

In Manila , I enjoyed the work as a journalist, quite ironical because I was a graduate of civil engineering and I had never taken up any journalism subject. All my journalistic knowledge were learned from KNCHS, as a student of a pretty teacher named "Miss Milna Bugante." But I performed the job with pride. In all these working years, my mind was focused on journalism and I loved that work. This made me forget my beloved in most of the days. I learned to drink liquor till the break of dawn every after work. I was always drunk. One reason why I always got drunk was my jilted heart, jilted because I had never gotten up to try to fulfill my dream to marry that girl of my love. The thought of her would crop up every time my mind would become tipsy from the wines. The next day, I would wake up rushing up for work again. The cycle repeated everyday in all those 14 years.

I found an eye on a few girls in Manila and I wondered why I was courageous enough to court them and be my girlfriends yet I cannot do the same to my beloved girl from KNCHS. Yes, I admit that I had some feelings for all those girls I courted. But I also admit that these feelings were not enough for me to decide to marry any of them.

One day I found myself bored of what I was doing day in and day out: work and drink. I decided to take up law to have some challenges. I did not want to become a lawyer, but I wanted to train my focus elsewhere for a new environment. So I took the entrance exam of Pamantasan ng Lungsod ng Maynila (PLM), which is so near from my place of work. I got a very high score and I was awarded a full scholarship. I concentrated on my studies and I abruptly stopped drinking. I finished the schooling in time in 2005 and passed the Bar Exams given the same year.

After the announcement of the Bar Exam results, drastic change happened in my life, professionally. I engaged myself in legal works and legal writing. My skills I acquired from being a journalist   sharpened   further.

I registered several feats in law works, winning almost all cases I handled. The one I consider as the best performance of my life is the petition I wrote to the Supreme Court asking for the application of the rule of preference in cases of conviction of journalists for libel. All the 15 justices voted to grant my petition on January 25, 2008. From then on, the trial courts were advised by the Highest Court not to imprison media men convicted of libel but impose only the fine of 6,000 pesos written under Article 355 of the Revised Penal Code as one of the three penalties that may be meted out. The first beneficiary of this feat of mine is movie writer Cristy Fermin; thereafter the hard-hitting Raffy Tulfo and his co-accused.

One thing that made this achievement so special to me is that it came to my mind while the press community had been at a loss for over 50 years on how to fight criminal libel that had been a real risk to the practice of the profession; they asked for help from many lawyers and none of them thought about what I did. I was praised to high heavens as "genius" and then awarded by National Press Club with a distinction for this legacy. Another thing that made this feat so special is the fact that I won it in a manner that is extraordinary: any petition to the Supreme Court is dead if there is no controversy, but my arguments proved compelling to become an exception to the general rule. The Highest Tribunal was criticized by authorities in law for it was not correct to act on a petition without an actual controversy and that the Supreme Court committed an act of virtual making of a law that should be the job of the Congress.

Other performances I consider as my best are my wins in all cases the GSIS filed against National Press Club and its officers, on issues springing from ownership of the land where the NPC Building stands. The said parcel of land has been registered in the name of GSIS. But my legal theories and arguments prevailed in courts. Now, the GSIS is appealing all those cases before the Court of Appeals.

My writing skills, admittedly, has separated me from the rest of legal minds. It is this and my passion to help people that have given me a very good name among my journalism peers in Metro Manila--and forget my dream girl for a while. Nevertheless, these feats are nothing compared to the dream about my true love, a dream that turned out now to have been doomed from the start.

Buoyant on these feats, I would come home to my hometown at least once a year to be present in each of a few grand reunions of KNCHS. In 2007 when Batch '82, my class, was the host, I was there and I was tapped by my batch mates as the instant master of ceremonies. I tried to deliver my best shot. I was glad I thought I delivered.

In almost all of those visits to my hometown, I would never fail to see my beloved for even just a glimpse. This time, she looked to me as one fine mature lady with a unique beauty. I still felt that strong feelings for her. In fact, I even visited her at her house in a few occasions, including that one when I showed my sympathy to their family over the loss of their mother and the first home visit where I was nearly bitten by their dog on my way out; thanks for she led me to their gate and she was there beside me to smoother the dog. How I felt so good about that very brief visit.

Nothing concrete happened for me to be able to lift my dream to near reality. Every time I would try to, I would chicken out into resignation and devastation -- although no longer as hurting as it was during my high school days.

I had tried several times to open up hoping she would reciprocate in order for me to go further. But nothing encouraging took place. The series of failures was never too much for me but these were enough for me to say I have already accepted it as fact of the matter: that we were never meant for each other. As far as I am concerned, that dream is now doomed from the start. I have been dreaming too long, for at least three decades, and I have never waken up to a reality. Perhaps, if I should dream of her again I should wake up right away to do a make-or-break move. But since I could not turn back the hands of time, that dream is now just another dream, by nature a world apart from reality.

But because she is my true love, I have pledged not to marry anymore -- till the end of time.

So that if I imagine again KNCHS were not born to exist, I could have been married to another woman.

This is my love story, a story that could have not been born were it not for KNCHS.

Without KNCHS: I could have not loved—and cried.

4 - 422 Years Ago

Rodel Rodis

Rodel Rodis is a lawyer and writer with his own blogsite. He is active member in several egroups. I thank him for the use of this article.

Dateline: INQUIRER.net First Posted 09:52:00 10/15/2009 Filed Under: CALIFORNIA, United States –

Historical records do not cite the names of any of the "Luzon Indios" aboard the Nuestra Senora de Buena Esperanza when it landed in Morro Bay, California on October 18, 1587.

All we know of the people who would later be called "Filipinos" was that the Esperanza's captain, Pedro De Unamuno, wrote in his log that his crew was composed of "Luzon Indios." All the natives of the Spanish colonies were called "Indios."

According to Unamuno's account, because his ship needed to replenish its supplies after two months at sea, he had to dock in the nearest land even if it was not found on any of the Spanish maps, a land that would later be called California.

Unamuno wrote that he sent two groups to explore the land, one group of 12 soldiers which he personally led, and a group of

Luzon Indios led by a Franciscan priest, Fr. Martin Ignacio De Loyola. Fr. Loyola carried a cross while his Indios were armed with swords and shields.

While reconnoitering the new land, the Luzon Indios encountered a group of five males, two females, and two babies that may similarly be called California Indios. But the natives ran from them to avoid any contact. Father De Loyola and his Indios then returned back to the Esperanza.

The following day, October 19, Unamuno ventured on shore again with 12 Spanish soldiers and eight Luzon Indios led this time by Fr. Francisco De Noguera. Two of the indios were sent ahead to scout the terrain. They found a camp with 17 dugouts of varying sizes that had just been abandoned by the natives who were eager to avoid contact. After failing to make contact with any of the natives, Unamuno and his crew then camped out.

While Unamuno and his crew were exploring the land, Fr. Martin and another crew of Luzon Indios went ashore to get wood and fresh water for the ship and to wash their clothes at a nearby creek. As they were doing so, a group of 23 natives approached them to ask them what they were doing. As there was a language problem, they could not understand each other. Because of their superior numbers, the natives were able to seize the clothes the Luzon Indios were washing and their water canteens. When they tried to seize Fr. Martin, gun shots came from the ship, forcing the natives to withdraw.

On Tuesday, October 20, Unamuno and his soldiers were nearing their ship when they saw two Luzon Indios running down from a hill, under attack from the natives. Unamuno's soldiers went up the hill to repulse the attackers. Three of his soldiers were wounded including one fatally. Unamuno reported that a Luzon Indio was also killed by "a javelin which he failed to ward off with his shield."

After a prolonged battle, Unamuno and his crew returned to the

Esperanza and decided to continue their voyage to Acapulco on October 21 reaching Acapulco on November 22, 1587.

It would take another eight years before another group of Filipinos would return to California.

On November 6, 1595, a Spanish galleon ship, the San Agustin, landed in what is now Point Reyes in Marin County in the San Francisco Bay Area. The Spaniards christened the bay "La Bahia de San Francisco" but it would take another century for the bay across from Point Reyes to be called that name.

In his San Francisco Chronicle article (400th Anniversary Of Spanish Shipwreck, November 14, 1995), Carl Nolte wrote "the San Agustin, which was probably a small warship in the Spanish navy, was commanded by Sebastian Rodriguez Cermeno and had a crew of Spanish officers and Filipino sailors, according to historian Raymond Aker, who has studied the ship and its voyage. The expedition turned out badly: The San Agustin was the first ship known to be wrecked on the California coast."

The San Agustin's voyage began in the summer of 1595 when it sailed from Manila to Acapulco with a cargo of 130 tons of Ming Dynasty porcelain, silk, and other trade goods from China bound for Spain. It was part of the Manila-Acapulco Galleon Trade that would dominate the economy of the Philippine colony from 1565 to 1815.

On occasion, a galleon ship would also carry gold and silver, extracted from Philippine mines. This was the case with the Santa Ana, a galleon ship that left Manila the year after Pedro De Unamuno's voyage, in 1588. It was hijacked by English pirates off the coast of Mexico.

When the San Agustin landed in Point Reyes, the ship's Spanish officers wanted to quickly resume the voyage to Acapulco but Captain Cermeno wanted to explore the land. By then the ship had made contact with the local natives, the Coast Miwoks, who lived in about six villages in the area. Cermeno gave them cloths and other gifts while the Miwoks gave them seeds and a banner of black feathers.

At Cermeno's direction, the Filipino sailors "assembled a small launch on the beach for exploring the shallow waters nearby. They stayed at the bay for three weeks, in gentle fall weather." Unfortunately, a storm came which pulled the ship's anchor up and blew the ship to the rocks, killing a dozen men including a priest.

What happened to the cargo of the San Agustin? According to Nolte, "The Miwoks picked up the cargo, slept on the silk meant for the royalty of Europe, ate from the priceless blue porcelain of the Wan Li period of the Ming Dynasty."

Captain Cermeno and his crew of Filipino sailors and a dog then built a larger launch from the materials they could find in Point Reyes and sailed out to Acapulco, which they reached without losing a man. They did lose the dog, though, which the Filipino crew and their Spanish captain ate to survive.

Please send comments to Rodel50@aol.com or mail them to the Law Offices of Rodel Rodis at 2429 Ocean Avenue, San Francisco, California 94127. For past columns, log on to Rodel50.blogspot.com.

5 - Filipino American History Month

Rodel Rodis

Rodel Rodis is a lawyer and writer with his own blogsite. He is active member in several egroups. I thank him for the use of this article.

Dateline, INQUIRER.net First Posted 09:03:00 11/05/2009 Filed Under: CALIFORNIA, United States —

If you google "Chinese American History Month" or "Japanese American History Month," the search engine will direct you to "Asian Pacific American Heritage Month," enacted into law on October 28, 1992 to honor the achievements of Asian/Pacific Americans and their contributions to the US.

All 30 or so Asian ethnic groups in the US were lumped together as "Asian Pacific Americans" and given one month (May) to celebrate their collective and individual cultures, histories, and heritage in the United States. The month of May was chosen because the first Japanese immigrants arrived in the United States on May 7, 1843 and the transcontinental railroad, which employed hundreds of Chinese immigrant laborers, was completed on May 10, 1869 (Golden Spike Day).

It actually started out as "Asian Pacific American Heritage Week" when President Jimmy Carter signed the Joint Resolution on October 2, 1978 but it became a month-long celebration in 1992 when President George H.W. Bush signed the law permanently designating May of each year as Asian Pacific American Heritage Month.

But Filipino Americans were never satisfied with being lumped together with other "Asian Pacific Americans" in celebrating May because for one, May's only significant event for Filipinos was when the US Navy destroyed the Spanish armada in Manila Bay on May 1, 1898, which victory paved the way for the US colonization of the Philippines.

As a publicly elected official in San Francisco for 18 years, I regularly attended the annual kick-off celebration of Asian Pacific American Heritage Month in San Francisco's City Hall. It would always be awkward for me when Japanese Americans would recount the day in May of 1843 when the first Japanese arrived in the US and Chinese Americans would celebrate the day in May of 1869 when the Chinese-built transcontinental railroad was completed and I could not celebrate that day in May of 1898 when Dewey destroyed the Spanish Fleet which later resulted in the US suppression of our Philippine independence. ("Hurray, we've been invaded and colonized!")

For years since its founding in Seattle, Washington in 1982, it was always the goal of the Filipino American National History Society (FANHS) for Filipino Americans to be given our very own month to celebrate our history and culture in the United States.

At its biennial national conference in 1988, FANHS members unanimously passed a resolution "to establish Filipino American History Month to be observed annually and nationally throughout the United States and its Territories during the Month of October commencing in the Year 1992 to mark the 405th Anniversary of the Presence of Filipinos in the Continental United States."

The resolution also believed that such a month-long celebration would be "a significant time to study the advancement of Filipino Americans in the history of the United States, as a favorable time of celebration, remembrance, reflection, and motivation, and as a relevant time to renew more efforts toward research, examination, and promulgation of Filipino American history and culture in order to provide an opportunity for all Americans to learn and appreciate more about Filipino Americans and their historic contributions to our nation, these United States of America."

Just as Japanese Americans could celebrate the day the first Japanese immigrants landed in California in May of 1843, Filipino Americans could now also proudly commemorate the day the first Filipinos ("Luzon Indios") landed in California on October 18, 1587, more than 33 years before the first English immigrants landed on Plymouth Rock in 1620.

Beginning in 1989, Filipino Americans began celebrating October as Filipino American History Month with celebrations and festivities throughout the US. Various states, aside from California and Hawaii, would routinely pass resolutions as Michigan Governor Jennifer Granhom did when she proclaimed "October 2006, as Filipino American Heritage Month in Michigan, and I encourage all citizens to recognize, applaud, and participate in this celebration of the many contributions made by Filipino Americans that enhance the quality of life in Michigan."

But the celebration in various states somehow just wasn't enough. As the Wikipedia entry on this subject noted, "October as Filipino American History Month has not yet attained the prestige of other similar minority celebrations, such as the Black History Month in February, Women's History Month in March, and the Asian Pacific American Heritage Month in May. This is evidenced by the fact that no United States Congress has ever resolved to recognize Filipino American History Month."

That Wikipedia entry now needs to be updated. On November 3, 2009, Representative Stephen Lynch (D-Massachusetts) stood up on the House floor to announce that on October 29, 2009, the House Oversight and Government Reform Committee had unanimously approved House Resolution 780 celebrating October as Filipino American History Month. It was originally sponsored by Rep. Bob Filner (D-California) with over 50 members of the House signing on as co-sponsors. Rep. Lynch also announced that the US Senate had unanimously passed a similarly worded resolution (S. 298) on October 1, 2009. He asked for the unanimous consent of the House to make the bill into law.

Before the vote could take place, Rep. Patrick McHenry (R-North Carolina) stood up and deplored the lack of substantive resolutions being passed by the House but joined Rep. Lynch in asking for the unanimous consent of the House for HR 780.

When the call was made for the vote, it was passed unanimously. October is now Filipino American History Month in the United States!

Please send comments to Rodel50@aol.com or mail to the Law offices of Rodel Rodis at 2429 Ocean Avenue, San Francisco, CA 94127 or call (415) 334-7800. For past columns, log on to Rodel50.blogspot.com.

6 - An Urgent Need For Reflection: The Onrushing Gloom In The Philippines

(An Open Letter to Mon Ramirez and the Powerful People in the Philippines and the World)

Cesar Torres

Cesar Torres is a well known Professor of Political Science at the University of the Philippines for many years. Now based in USA, continues to advocate political reforms in the home country via internet.

Dateline, April 11, 2005

Dear Mon:
It has been a long time since I have read expressions such as "internal contradictions", etc. which you mentioned in one of your emails. I was familiar with concepts like this when I was with Polly Sigh. But not anymore.

There was something I remember also, Che Guevarra's admonition, i.e., "A guerilla should be like a fish in the water." So I would not be surprised if there are NDF cadres in Dasmarinas Village or Forbes Park. Commitment to our people can transcend social and economic origins. We once visited the compound of the Sisons in the Ilocos. His family origin is not exactly similar to those surviving on garbage like those Filipinos in Payatas.

One does not need to be a Ph.D. in "revolutionary movements" to know that the inability of a political and government system to provide the basic needs of the people -- I don't need to detail them here -- is the compelling reason why people rebel. In the context of the Philippines, we know that the problems are massive. My relatives are constantly crying to me for help. And we know that the NPA and the RHB guerillas are not lugging those corroded arms in the hinterlands because they like doing that.

The world is in crisis. It is not only the Filipinos who are suffering. Even the Americans, and possibly, the Japanese, the Europeans and other countries belonging to the "First World". The tragedy of 9-11 has resulted in this world crisis. You are giving too much power to Gloria if you tell me that the misery of my relatives and my fellow Filipinos are just the result of Gloria and her group's incompetence and mishandling of the Philippine problems.

I can grant that more and more people will be marching in the streets, their left fists raised and shouting all those slogans that have been popular when the Beloved Warrior was contemplating the loveliness of the various UP co-eds at the back of the UP Main Library and wondering why there were a lot of squatters in Tondo, who were mostly from Samar. There were no Smokey Mountains yet, and no garbage-subsisting Filipinos in Payatas.

All those red flags can be unfurled. And the anger of our people will be dramatized on TV, and published in the periodicals. The natural course of events will eventually result in more and more people being bloodied. More and more people probably joining the revolutionary groups for the sake of survival because they cannot run to the police, and the military, and the court system for justice and protection. More and more clashes will happen in the mountains of Samar and other parts of the Philippines. More will die.

Who knows, that "strategic offensive" might indeed happen. One does not need to read MTT or the Beloved Warrior's "Philippine Society and Revolution" to know that this has always been the natural course of events since the dawn of mankind.

Anyway, considering the dream society that we are longing for and which the NDF has been longing for and which the CPP says will eventually be attained because it is "inevitable", frankly I am afraid that it could just result in the "Killing Fields" and the "Mountains of Skulls" similar to what happened in Cambodia, in Rwanda, in Somalia, and perhaps in Colombia.

The Vietnamese liberation forces and in the neighboring countries triumphed. My pedestrian thinking tells me that the conditions where ripe. Remember Lenin's "confluence of events" explaining why the Russian Revolution triumphed in the 1920's?

Remember how the USSR and Eastern Europe and the People's Republic of China joined forces to fight US intervention in Vietnam?

Remember how millions of Americans and millions more all over the world organized to stop that miserable war in Indochina?

Today, we cannot even point out to a "successful socialist society" that will inspire the cannon fodders of the revolution, our poor Filipino masses, who will be the first ones to die if the hoped-for civil war is going to intensify.

Are we going to tell them about the collapse of the USSR and the other socialist societies in Europe? How about the debacle of the FSLN in Nicaragua? Are we going to tell them about the hunger in socialist North Korea and the aberration of their leader? Perhaps we can talk about Cuba, or even the PRC with its weird economic system or Vietnam whose economy is being dominated by American and European multinationals.

And you will not forget that in the Index of Corruption, it seems there is more corruption in Vietnam and PRC than in Singapore and other non socialist societies in Asia.

And then if the Philippine military, egged on and supported by the warmongers in America, will intensify their experiments on the effectiveness of their weapons, will the American public, its religious groups like those who elected GWB to a second term, in sympathy and solidarity with the 3 million or so Filipinos in America demand that the killings of the peasants
in the Philippines stop?

The Filipinos in America are a mystery to me. Many of them will curse Filipinos who will say anything unflattering about American foreign and economy policy in the Philippines. They don't want to rock the boat. They don't want to call attention to themselves, especially the "successful" ones.

Will the Europeans who are not at all mesmerized by American foreign and economic policies demand that the EU tell the Philippine military to stop its killings of the Filipinos?

Will the 1.2 billion Chinese and their ruling group intervene to stop the killings of the Filipinos?

How about the Catholic Church? After all the CBCP is being targeted as an "enemy" of the friends of Gen. Carlos Garcia. Will the new Pontiff excommunicate the Catholic Generals who are directing the poor Filipino soldiers to seek out and kill their fellow poor Filipinos? The generals will just laugh or imprison the priests.

Will the NDF be supported by the fanatics in Al Qaeda and Jemaah Islamiyah in exchange for detaching Mindanao and Sulu from Luzviminda? Are they really serious about this?

Mon, the world is in crisis. And it is intensifying in the Philippines.

My plea, and many of my colleagues in Samar share my prayer, is for the armed groups to stop their obsession to kill, especially if they are not the ones being hunted or directly doing the killing, like those poor soldiers and the NPA guerillas in the mountains of Samar and other places of the Philippines.

Our resources can be used to feed our people, educate them so that they are skilled, and are nationalists, so that they get cured when they are sick, so that they can have a better future.

Take this example for instance. In the interior of Samar, in the town of San Jose de Buan, the children had no toilet. No books, no laboratory equipment. There is supposed to be a complete elementary school and a high school in that town. Their elected municipal leaders are not even staying in the town. They are getting their salaries as officials, but what are they doing?

The irony is that there is probably a military garrison there with soldiers and guns. True, they have been conducting adult literacy classes in Samar. But how much is one armalite for instance? And since San Jose de Buan is in the interior of Samar, and the area is ideal for guerilla warfare, perhaps the NDF partisans and their enemies the RHB armed group are maintaining some presence there. They would have guns too. How much is one armalite whether in the hand of a Government soldier or an NPA or RHB figther?

Two armalites would be enough to construct a comfort room, buy books, and laboratory equipment for the children in San Jose de Buan.

And if the powerful people in the Philippines had their priorities in order, the NPAs and the Government soldiers can plant trees in the denuded mountains of Samar and the Philippines. Instead of playing hide and seek ambushing each other. They can work together to repair the miserable public roads in the Philippines. Look what my townmates in Villareal, Samar are doing.

Or they can join Gawad Kalinga in building houses for our people who are residing under the bridges or have squatted in cemeteries and catacombs. Or they can maintain the fish sanctuaries all over the Philippines.

I think the leadership of the NDF should pause and re-evaluate its position with respect to attaining a more progressive and respectable Philippines. Perhaps, we can learn from the Tupamaros in Uruguay. They are no longer pursuing their cherished principles and ideals while shooting government soldiers. Satur Ocampo, Walden Bello, Akbayan, the CBCP, etc. can provide the balance to the corrupt and the incompetent power holders in Philippine society. As a friend in embattled Mindanao said: "Sana naman hindi na lang puna ng puna. Dapat mayroon ipakita na viable alternative."

Mon, I think many of us are very, very proud Filipinos. Many of us are willing to die for Pilipinas. But I don't think they are ready to die for Fernando Poe and Susan Roces or for poor Erap and his mistresses or for the No. 1 UP alumnus so that he can maintain his place in Transparency International and ensure that his love child in Australia will be a multimillionaire for life or for the super rich Atenista or for the fanatics of Al Qaeda.

Many have second thoughts that only through a "protracted war" can we offer a better life for our people. The sacrifices are just mind-boggling. And it may take generations for us to recover, if we will be able to recover at all.

And what's more, we will be lying to ourselves and to the Filipino people.

I remember a sad story being told to me of an idealist who went to the mountains but is now back in the "lowlands". To inspire the peasants, he would tell them: "Kasama, nasa Malakanyang na tayo sa dalawang taon." And the poor peasant believed him. That was more than 20 years ago. And the poor peasant and his family? They were wiped out.

"Pragmatic Nationalism" and a "Government of National Reconciliation", Mon. Let us think about this.

Let the powers that be request Dr. Jose Abueva and think tank groups -- such as the Development Academy of the Philippines, that National Defense College, Ibon, the PCIJ, CBCP, the Institute of Islamic Studies -- to present a workable concept paper to Malacanang, to the Congress, to the White House (in case they are thinking of unloading more of their unused weapons to the Philippine military as "foreign aid"), to the NDF, to Akbayan, to the MILF and to the Catholic Church. Let us see what happens. But get the assent of the leaders of these organizations. And let the killings stop.

This can become a foundation for a "Government of National Reconciliation". And we can move on.

Otherwise, the alternatives are terrifying. As someone in Talsik@yahoogroups.com keeps on saying: "War! War! War! War!"

7 - Did Ninoy Die For Nothing

Joey Concepcion

Joey Concepcion is the son of the famous head of Namfrel Mr. Jose Concepcion for several decades. Joey is also the grandson of Don Salvador Araneta. Joey is now the President of RFM Corporation. He is also advocate of entrepreneuship via his "gonegosyo" website and his writings.

August 21, 2008 marked the 25th death anniversary of Benigno "Ninoy" Aquino Jr. After so many years, it still brings back a lot of memories, having spent most of my teenage years during the martial law days.

Many people don't know that our family never applied for Canadian residency during those times. While my cousins on both sides of the family left the country, we were left here. We had to deal with a very dangerous environment, since my father was a strong advocate for democracy. My grandfather, Salvador Araneta, was in Canada like many others in exile for fear that they would be sent to jail.

When martial law was declared, my father, who was a con-con delegate, was also one of those who were imprisoned. I remember hiding in my uncle's house in Batangas and some family friends' house in the village. One night, our house was surrounded by military men. My mother woke us up and told us that my dad was going to be detained in Camp Crame. On the day that we were allowed to speak to my dad through a wall with a screen, I remember writing a letter and saying bad things about Marcos, being a very young child at that time. Because of that, I was questioned by the military. I didn't know they would be reading those letters. I was only about 14 years old at that time.

Sundays at Camp Crame was different. It was hot. We stayed in a gym, where there were only electric fans. With my dad in Crame were other political detainees like Max Soliven, Bren Guiao and Sonny Alvarez. I remember people playing badminton. After a while the guards were nicer. When my dad had to visit my lolo who was in the hospital, he had to get special permission from Enrile at that time. My grandparents did not know that he was in jail until much later.

These were the beginnings that I guess motivated my father to fight for justice and see the Philippine democracy succeed. My father started NAMFREL when most people gave up hope. He lit the first candle of hope. Organizing NAMFREL at that time was challenging, having people like Christian and Winnie Monsod, Raul Roco, Ting Jaime, Jaime Ferrer, Ching Escaler, Teresa Nieva and others who were all independent-minded Filipinos and strong in character. My father was able to bring together the best in NAMFREL. From there, so many candles of hope were lit.

NAMFREL was crucial during 1984 elections. Being my father's sidekick, I was with him even in my teens. I remember going through different barangays with our bodyguards and still being chased by goons.

Filipinos who wanted to be part of change joined NAMFREL and risked their own lives to fight for democracy. At that time, my father's banner color even during the concon days was already yellow. His eyeglasses matched that of Ninoy Aquino's big black glasses, which by the way is now back in fashion.

My father's best interview was that of TV host Ronnie

Nathanielz, who was with a Marcos-run station. That interview strengthened NAMFREL's cause. Later, we saw history unfold. The poll watchers walked out of PICC when they were being asked to adjust the election results. NAMFREL started what was going to be known as the people power revolution. The candle that was lit continued until the Edsa revolution.

Ninoy's decision to come home was part of his destiny. He knew that something was going to happen once he came back, but he also knew that he had to come back. When his son, Noynoy Aquino, mentioned that since his father's death, nothing had changed, I felt I had to write this column.

Many things have changed for the better. First we have a democracy, and we have a very much active Congress, both Senate and the House. People can speak out what they want to say. We see investigations happening left and right. Our press is also free. One cannot compare it during those days when we had only government stations. We have a young but working democracy,

People like Ninoy and Joecon taught us the need to give hope and take control of our destiny. They did not lose hope. They lit that candle that gave courage to millions of Filipinos to go and watch the ballots, and eventually, to march for freedom. One is not just entitled to luck; one has to work for it.

Seeing political and economic progress takes generations and lifetimes. While poverty and corruption still exists, we see more people taking action towards improvement. The OFW workers, who leave the Philippines and sacrifice for their families, are taking control of their future. Call center agents, who work at night and sacrifice lifestyle change, also take control of their future. Somehow, in our small way, Go Negosyo is all about continuing what great men and women have started. It is continuing to light the candle of hope.

Economic progress will happen to those who want it and work for it. It is a matter of attitude. It does not necessarily mean one has to have a negosyo to be prosperous. Its is the entrepreneurial attitude that sees opportunities in every crisis, solutions to problems, and those working hard for something and taking better control of their future. Those people who sacrifice living abroad are not waiting for luck. They are creating luck because they work for it. I definitely have to say Ninoy's death was not a waste. He, for many, is our modern day hero. As my father would say, "it is better to light the candle than curse the darkness". Let there be more modern day heroes who will bring the correct attitude that will finally bring prosperity to this nation. Success will not be dependent on the next president in 2010, but it will be dependent on more and more Filipinos who are willing to do something about their future.

8 – Criteria on Charity Organizations

American Institute of Philanthropy (AIP)

Courtesy of AIP that granted permission to reprint CRITERIA a major article at their website, http://www.charitywatch.org/ Readers are encouraged to explore more information therein in order to educate themselves on which charity organizations are highly rated and poorly rated. It is earnestly hoped that the same criteria be adopted on charitable organizations and foundations in the Philippines.

Selecting a charity to support is a bit like playing God. Ideally, it should take into account your most deeply held concerns and convictions.

Before sending in a donation to a group, you can now consider how well it will spend your money by referring to the AIP's *Charity Rating Guide*. Each organization is listed by category with its phone number, financial performance measurements and an overall grade (where enough information is available). You can also review the ratings of other charities in the same category to compare a particular group with those which do similar work.

The *Guide* indicates whether or not an organization is eligible to receive tax-deductible contributions, noting those charities which may have separately incorporated entities with a different tax-deductibility status.

The *Guide* shows which groups are new or have received an updated evaluation.

The *Guide* shows which groups have provided AIP the following documents (which we have requested): annual report, complete audited financial statements and Internal Revenue Service form 990 with Schedule A where applicable. Donors may want to consider an organization's accountability to AIP when making giving decisions.

Omission of charities from the *Charity Rating Guide* or this web site does not imply a negative evaluation or rating.

Some groups receive large amounts of donated goods and services. These items can be difficult to value and distort the calculation of how efficiently a charity is spending your dollars. Donated items are generally excluded from AIP's calculation of the following ratios:

PERCENT SPENT ON CHARITABLE PURPOSE

This is the portion of total expenses that is spent on charitable programs. In AIP's view, 60% or greater is reasonable for most charities. The remaining percentage is spent on fundraising and general administration. **Note:** A 60% program percentage typically indicates a "satisfactory" or "C range" rating. Most highly efficient charities are able to spend 75% or more on programs.

When a range of numbers is given, the higher number, in most cases, reflects the charity's own decision on how much is spent on charitable program expenses. The mailings and phone calls of these groups may serve a dual purpose: raising funds and educating donors. However many of these groups consider such mailings and phone calls to be largely educational and their costs to be primarily program expenses. In some cases AIP adjusts the higher number. For example, AIP may differ with a group's decision that the cost of acquiring new donors or members is a program service. Fundraising costs, i.e., direct mail and telemarketing, are often factored in as program expenses. If you agree that fundraising activities serve as a bona-fide educational or program purpose, you may decide that this higher number reflects your goals.

The lower AIP number assumes that all direct mail telemarketing and solicitation costs are *separate* fund-raising expenses and should not be included with direct program service costs. If you do not consider any portion of a charity's direct mail and telemarketing solicitations to be a bona-fide program or if you are a new contributor and do not want to fund solicitation campaigns, the lower number reflects your goals. (The AIP letter grade ratings are based on this assumption.) Please note, however, that the work done by certain types of nonprofit organizations may warrant a greater allocation of direct mail and telemarketing costs to program expenses. Please see "Exception for Social Welfare Groups" below for more details.

COST TO RAISE $100

This dollar amount reflects how much is spent to raise each $100 of funds collected. In AIP's view, $35 or less to raise $100 is reasonable for most charities. When a range is given, the lower amount usually reflects the charity's own decision on how much direct mail and telemarketing costs are bona-fide fundraising expenses. In some cases, AIP adjusts the lower number to reflect its different view on whether an item is a fundraising expense. The higher AIP number assumes that *all* (please see "Exceptions for Social Welfare Groups" below) direct mail and telemarketing solicitation costs are fund-raising expenses.

AIP helps you to judge the fundraising efficiency of a charity by comparing fund-raising expense with related contributions, i.e., money that was brought in as a result of fundraising activities; whereas many charities compare (by pie charts or ratios) their cost to raise money with total income, which can include patient revenue, investment income, sales proceeds and other items that are not affected by fundraising outlays. This erroneous comparison often makes a charity's fundraising efficiency appear better than it actually is. The following comparison illustrates this point:

Erroneous Comparison:

$100,000 Fundraising Expense/ $1,000,000 Total Income = 10/100 = 10%

Using this formula, a charity can claim that only 10% of its total income was spent on fundraising. This percentage may look great in a charity's promotional material but it is not a meaningful measurement of fund-raising efficiency.

AIP Comparison:

$100,000 Fundraising expense/ $200,000 Related Contributions = 50/100 = 50%

Using this formula, one can see that Charity X has a fund-raising efficiency of 50% or that it costs the charity $50 to raise $100. This ratio is useful because it tells donors how much a charity is spending to obtain your contribution and how much is left to spend on charitable programs and general administration.

EXCEPTION FOR SOCIAL WELFARE GROUPS

The mailings and phone calls of social welfare groups that are not eligible to receive tax-deductible contributions, identified by the "nt" designation in the *Charity Rating Guide*, may serve a dual purpose: raising funds and recruiting/educating members to write their congressman or make other attempts to influence legislation. AIP counts up to 30% of the cost of such mailings and phone calls as program expenses in its lower number for "% Spent on Charitable Purpose," its higher number for "cost to raise $100" and its overall grade. Please note however, that many of these groups consider such mailings and phone calls to be largely educational and allocate over 30% of these costs to program expenses. These accounting differences may cause lower overall grades for some social welfare organizations.

YEARS OF AVAILABLE ASSETS
This column shows how long a charity with large reserves of available assets could continue to operate at current levels

without any additional fundraising. In AIP's view, a reserve of less than three years is reasonable and does not affect a group's grade. When years of available assets are 3 years or more, they are shown in a separate chart.

GRADE

The letter grades for most charities are based on "% Spent On Charitable Purpose" and "Cost to Raise $100," and assumes that direct mail and telemarketing solicitations are fund-raising costs. (Please see "Exception for Social Welfare Groups" above.) When a charity's years of available assets are three years or more, their grade is reduced and reported in a separate chart.

Groups with "years of available assets" of more than five years are the "least needy" in AIP's view, and receive an "F" grade regardless of other measurements. (Please see "Charities with Large Asset Reserves" below.)

AIP encourages each donor to consider these factors and others, which you may feel are more significant, when making charitable giving decisions. AIP provides this information to help you make your own decision concerning which charity to support. The letter grades represent the *opinion* of AIP.

A charity's rating is based solely on the above criteria. The grades are:

A = Excellent
B = Good
C = Satisfactory
D = Unsatisfactory
F = Poor ? = Insufficient Information

When information is given only on the national headquarters and the charity does not include its affiliates in its financial statements, "National Office" or "N.O." appears after the group's name.

GRADE CHANGES

Does a charity's grade fluctuate much? Usually new evaluations of charities do not result in more than a letter grade change, though it is important to regularly check the grades of your favorite charities because there are exceptions. For example, the grade of **United States Association for UNHCR** (United Nations High Commissioner for Refugees) went from **A-** to **D** to **C** to **B** to **C** over a several year period.

CHARITIES WITH LARGE ASSET RESERVES

AIP strongly believes that your dollars are most urgently needed by charities that do not have large reserves of available assets. AIP therefore *reduces* the grade of any group that has available assets equal to three to five years of operating expenses. In AIP's view, a reserve of less than three years is reasonable and does not affect a group's grade.

These reductions in grades are based *solely* on the charities' asset reserves as compared to budget. If you agree with these charities that reserves greater than three years' budget are necessary to enhance their long-term stability, you may wish to disregard the lower grades that AIP assigns on the basis of high assets.

AIP's definition of "years of available assets" includes funds currently available for the charity's use, including investments that the charity has set aside as a reserve but could choose to spend if it wanted to do so.

CATHOLIC CHARITIES, UNITED WAY, VOLUNTEERS OF AMERICA AND UNITED JEWISH COMMUNITIES

These groups are composed of hundreds of local organizations. Each of these is governed by local volunteers and primarily raises and spends money in their own community. AIP's *Charity Rating Guide* currently focuses on national organizations.

HOW TO LEARN MORE

After selecting your favorite charities, you can call or write to them for a description of their mission, program activities and recent accomplishments. (Phone numbers are provided in the *Charity Rating Guide* and addresses can be found on the Internet or in the reference sections of most public libraries.) Insist that the descriptions of program activities be clear and quantifiable (for example, How many hungry were fed? or How much land was protected?) and coincide with the time period and categories of the financial statements.

WORDS OF CAUTION

Charity financial reporting is inconsistent, unclear and often incorrect. To form a basis of comparison, adjustments have been made to the financial reports of some of the organizations in this guide. For example, if a charity does a lot of direct mail soliciting but includes only a small portion of its total postage and printing in fund-raising expenses, then AIP's rating will reflect a larger share of these items in fundraising.

Hot Topics | Top-Rated | A–Z Listing | Criteria | Tips | FAQ | Articles | About AIP | Rating Guide | Links | Praise | Membership | Contact | Home
(Above are the sections in their website for further exploration by the readers.)

American Institute of Philanthropy
3450 N. Lake Shore Dr. Ste. 2802
P.O. Box 578460
Chicago, IL 60657
773.529.2300 (phone)
773.529.0024 (fax)
aipmail@charitywatch.org
www.charitywatch.org

9 - The Coming Revolution
In The Ballot Box

Cesar Lumba

About the author: Taken from his blogsite,
http://www.nykos2.blogspot.com
In his own words: From Las Vegas, Nevada. People know me as a
serious senior citizen who wants to give back to the world that has given
him so much in life. I really am attracted to the great causes and issues
of good citizenship. What people don't generally know about me is that I
have a good sense of humor. I laugh at myself a lot, I have fun thinking
of the most ordinary, mundane things. I am not a quick wit, so I can't be
an impromptu comic, but I usually find humor in my after-the-fact
reflections. This, I guess, makes me qualified to write a blog about
humor in our daily lives.

Dateline, Dec. 2009.

My friends inform me that any attempt to cause a change in
the way Filipinos elect their leaders is doomed from the start.

"Filipinos will always elect those who give them the most money,
who promise them jobs, who spring for that goiter surgery that
some voters need from time to time," my friends tell me, "even -
and perhaps especially - if the candidates they elect are corrupt

and routinely send out their goons to force their will on the public."

It's just the way it is, my friends tell me.

And, my friends are right. Philippine democracy is a big joke. People do not embrace the concept of the greater good. There's only the personal good, or the welfare of the extended family to think of. The country be damned, it's damned anyway already.

Why is Philippine culture so everyone-to-himself, the-country-be-damned? There are several theories about this. One theory is that the Philippines is made up of 7100 islands and each large island or island chain developed over time into a separate nation. The provincial, or the parochial psyche developed and went into full bloom, while the nation remained an elusive ideal, a chimera.

The second theory is poli-cultural, i.e., both political and cultural. In Nick Joaquin's famous essay, he bemoans the fact that the country's culture is a culture of exploitation. One is either an exploiter or the exploited. One's job and lifetime preoccupation is to remain an exploiter if already one, or become an exploiter if not one already. Those in government exploit the citizens and do not serve them.

The third may be the explanation for the second. The landed gentry in the Philippines, which became the aristocracy in the vastly agricultural Philippines during the Spanish era, were installed by the Spanish crown, notoriously by Queen Isabela, who granted her favorites large tracts of land in the Philippines. These royal grants created a European-style feudal system that forced the native populations into a position of servility vis-a-vis the feudal lords who were supported by the Spanish crown through the dreaded Guardia Civil. Unlike in the wild west of the United States, where adventurous Americans acquired properties through homesteading and commercial acumen, the native inhabitants of what would eventually become the Philippines almost suddenly woke up to find that large tracts of land that they might have hunted on and might have cultivated now belonged to powerful feudal lords, as mandated by the Spanish monarchs. The distinction between the Philippine experience and the American West experience is, of course, an oversimplification. The native Americans (Indians) were in fact deprived of their hunting lands by the hordes of frontiersmen and women looking for land and gold, with the U.S. Federal government serving as brutal enablers.

Over nearly 400 years of Spanish colonial times, the native populations in the Philippines became wards of the owners of the big plantations and eventually became so dependent on those owners that they surrendered even their thinking processes to them.

The natives learned not to think for themselves; they depended on the big bosses, the big landowners to think for them.

By late 19th century, the winds of change were already howling, and a new intelligentsia class had begun to challenge the social order. This intelligentsia class, schooled in Spain and trained in the intellectual concepts of European Masonry - most of the Philippine revolutionaries were Masons - rebelled from the Spanish-installed aristocracy and friars and successfully erected the first Philippine Republic on June 12, 1898.

The new revolutionary government, however, never actually sat in power. The emerging interventionist global American power intervened and the Philippine-American war of attrition began.

Much of the Philippines was unaffected by what was going on in Manila. Much of the Philippines was still feudal, exploitative, provincial, parochial and clannish. Throughout the rest of the Philippines, the Manila government - now run by Americans - was for the most part a foreign power.

The Americans introduced Filipinos to American-style democracy, but it seems that they were content to democratize only those in Manila and the surrounding areas. The rest of the country remained feudal. Examples of American modus operandi are today's Afghanistan, where the Americans have democratized Kabul and other important cities, but not the great Afghan countryside, which is ruled by warlords and the Taliban.

These were the conditions that were present at the time of the Philippine independence from the U.S. in 1946. Not much has changed. People in the provinces still vote for the candidates who can give them the most money, who can promise jobs for relatives, who come with medicines in times of need.

The idea that people should vote for those candidates who are projected to do good for the country is still alien to them. Their likely reply to entreaties from people like me is: "Define what's good for the country" or "Define country."

This may no longer be true in the not-too-distant future, however. In many cities and towns of the Philippines, local leaders and intellectuals schooled in Manila, Cebu, Davao and other major cities, are already trained - have long been trained - in thinking in terms of what's good for the country.

The recent voters' revolt in Pampanga, which installed a lowly and most unlikely priest as governor, is the strongest hint yet that Filipinos are waking up to the need for good leaders. Before that, the election of Estrada demonstrated that the common tao - the drivers, maids, sidewalk vendors, farmers and slum dwellers - would buck their masters to embrace a politician who vowed to fight for the welfare of the downtrodden and dispossessed.

While nothing seems to ever change in the Philippines, there are strong hints that the country is on the cusp of revolutionary upheavals in its electoral process. The groundwork has been set for a coming revolution in the ballot box.

While the intelligentsia and patriots never win elections, there is evidence that someday they will be racking up big, important wins. This despite contraindications in many small towns and municipalities, where people are still falling in love with the most popular and highly-visible personalities such as actors, TV hosts and boxers like Manny Pacquiao.

What this all means is that the electorate is becoming neurotic. Changes are happening quickly, unexpectedly. Voters are telling their political bosses that they themselves must determine the leaders who will receive their votes. Unfortunately, their choices have made things worse for the country and not a whit of difference for them. They are still dirt poor and their only salvation now is a one-way ticket out of the country. People do not understand why.

People are conflicted over the presidential election of 2004, when the clearly superior candidate Gloria Arroyo may have lost to the clearly inferior but supremely popular candidate, Fernando Poe, Jr., but allegedly resorted to widespread cheating to emerge the "victor."

Mrs. Arroyo, apparently stung by accusations of electoral fraud, seemingly lost all interest in appearing virtuous and is allegedly ruling as a corrupt and ruthless tyrant whose political moves consist of laying the groundwork for escaping prosecution once out of office.

First there was complete surrender of their democracy to the whims and caprices of their masters. Now, Filipino voters are beginning to break loose from their masters' hold and asserting their right to choose their destiny. Unfortunately, they are exercising this right by choosing the most inept, corrupt and unqualified candidates.

Philippine elections have become, for the most part, a joke. So why do I assume that it is possible to convince Filipinos to suddenly adopt a concept that is completely foreign to them: the idea that the public officials they elect are responsible to them, and that if those public officials do not do a good job, they - the people - must fire those officials.

I do not know that the coming Revolution in the Ballot Box is real or an illusion. I do not know that any efforts on my part to help this coming revolution along would yield any actual benefits. What I do know is that if not enough people pool their energies to help it along and focus that energy, it could fizzle, die on the vine.

Over the years a lot of Filipinos in the intellectual and elite classes have tried to educate Filipino voters to vote for the most qualified, not the most popular or the most generous with their ill-gotten wealth.

Most have failed. There is a very strong possibility that I will fail and others will fail. I'm in the bettors' paradise of Las Vegas, and I know that the odds for this coming Revolution in the Ballot Box that I'm talking about are in million to one territory.

But what if the idea of the Revolution in the Ballot Box catches fire on the Internet? What if enough people forward it and it makes the rounds in the Philippines and in the diaspora several times over? What if people actually take this call to arms seriously?

It is a simple concept. Do not vote for a re-electionist candidate. Vote for the most qualified opponent. Do it in protest. Scream from the rooftops that you are tired of incompetent and corrupt officials. You want justice, you want a future for your children. You want to live in the Philippines and not have to work as a maid or day laborer in some foreign land. You want to be safe from floods, from mudslides, from the rubble of buildings that collapse because they are not built to withstand medium-strength earthquakes.

You don't have to go through hoops or take extraordinary measures. Just don't vote for the incumbent public officials in your town, in your province, in the national government. Vote for

their   opponents.
And keep doing it until a new class of politicians emerge that serve you and serve you well, and do not have their hand in the collection box.

If the corrupt and incompetent politicians offer you money, take it but do not vote for them. They have been deceiving you all this time. Deceive them back. They are mostly Machiavellians; be a Machiavellian yourself. Deceive the deceivers.

If you keep doing this enough times, starting in May, 2010, someday - 20 to 30 years from now - you or your children will wake up and find a new Philippines being run by elected officials who serve their constituents well, who work for the public interest, who do not steal from the government.

That is what Revolution in the Ballot Box means.

10 - 2009 - A Retrospective

Cesar Lumba

About the author: Taken from his blogsite,
http://www.nykos2.blogspot.com
In his own words: From Las Vegas, Nevada. People know me as a serious senior citizen who wants to give back to the world that has given him so much in life. I really am attracted to the great causes and issues of good citizenship. What people don't generally know about me is that I have a good sense of humor. I laugh at myself a lot, I have fun thinking of the most ordinary, mundane things. I am not a quick wit, so I can't be an impromptu comic, but I usually find humor in my after-the-fact reflections. This, I guess, makes me qualified to write a blog about humor in our daily lives.

Dateline, Dec. 26, 2009

The year 2009 ends in a few days and with this year-end the first decade of the 21st century ends. In all the years I have been privileged to exist on this planet - or anywhere, as far as I know - there has never been a year when so many have disappointed nearly all of us.

If you are a thinking man with blood pressure problems, don't live in the Philippines for surely your elevated blood pressure will rocket through the ceiling. Don't live in the U.S. either, where the

Lords of Chutzpah held a never-ending Shriners-style convention all year. Don't live anywhere in the world, except perhaps Australia, Switzerland and Canada, where people seemed to get most things right.

I am creating year-end awards this year that I hope to keep up over the years. Luckily, there are some "points of light" in the heavenly darkness which leads one to conclude that there may be hope yet.

The Nykos2 Person of the Year: The deposed governor of Isabela province, Philippines -

Maria Gracia Cielo "Grace" Magno Padaca

The 46-year-old Grace Padaca, a recipient of the prestigious Ramon Magsaysay award for public service in 2008 and the International Women of Courage Award in 2007, was stripped of her governorship after the Philippines' Commission on Elections held a "recount" of votes that found Benjamin Dy had actually won the 2007 election for governor of Isabela. More than 17,000 votes previously counted for Governor Grace were invalidated by the Commission on Elections, First District, because Governor Padaca's name had been mis-spelled, yada-yada-yada.

The shenanigans employed by her opponents in the Comelec were reminiscent of the "hanging chads" controversy in the U.S. Presidential election (Gore vs. Bush) in 2000.

In the U.S. election, the question of voter intent was paramount, according to the Florida Supreme Court. If there was a clear indication that voters had selected either Bush or Gore, the votes should be counted even if the chads were hanging, indented, etc.

In the case of Benjamin Dy vs. Padaca in the Philippines, voters had clearly voted for Governor Padaca even though those voters had mis-spelled her name. Mystifyingly, the Comelec, First

District, invalidated those ballots and thus awarded the governorship to Benjamin Dy.

Mr. Dy apparently does not think that if there is a rematch he will prevail over Governor Grace, which is why he is running for mayor of his hometown instead of governor next year. Governor Grace will again run for governor and will probably win by a landslide. The Dy in the Dy dynasty who will be Governor Grace's opponent is the one who defeated her in 2001 for Congress, Faustino "Bojie" Dy. Ms. Padaca initially won that election, but her win was overturned by the House of Representatives Electoral Tribunal after votes marked only with "Grace" were invalidated even though no other person going by the name of "Grace" had run in that election.

Governor Grace Padaca, or simply "Grace" to her supporters, was a green revolutionist who stopped all the illegal logging that was going on in her province. She was a fighter for good governance and a passionate advocate of true democracy, which abhors dynasties. She openly campaigned against the dynastic stranglehold of Isabela politics by the Dy clan.

This created for her some very powerful enemies which eventually led to her downfall. She is an environmental and good governance martyr.

Courage and Conscience Awards

1. Governor Ed Panlilio of Pampanga, Philippines - a potential martyr for the cause of good governance. His election in 2007 is also under protest and may be overturned by the Commission on Elections. There is widespread apprehension that the Comelec may yet find a way to "sell" their looming decision to the public.

2. Naga City, Philippines Mayor Jesse Robredo - a good governance advocate allied with Governors Grace Padaca and Ed Panilio.

3. San Isidro, Nueva Ecija, Philippines Mayor Sonia Lorenzo - a good governance ally of Panilio, Padaca and Robredo.

4. Senator Harry Reid of Nevada, U.S.A. - once he had his jaws locked on health care reform in the U.S., he would not let go. His advocacy of the health care reform issue may yet turn out to be the final straw that will cost him his job as U.S. Senator in 2010. This was a sacrifice that he was obviously willing to make.

5. President Barack Obama - He used all of his political capital, and then some, to push through the unpopular stimulus package, the bailout of banks and the U.S. automobile industry, caps and trade, climate change and the health reform package in the U.S. Congress. All this at the risk of becoming a one-term President. A real stand-up "Profiles in Courage" guy.

6. The Christian Brothers (De La Salle Brothers) in the Philippines - They were the first mainstream religious group to condemn the Maguindanao massacre and to lay the blame at the feet of President Gloria Arroyo for coddling the alleged perpetrators, the Ampatuans. No other major religious group in the Philippines has had the courage to point out what is obvious to a lot of Filipinos, that the close ties between President Arroyo and the Ampatuans were partly responsible for the heinous crimes allegedly committed by the Ampatuans.

And now for the sad stories of 2009:

Sons and Daughters of Beelzebub Awards

1. Andal Ampatuan, Sr., Governor of Maguindanao Province, Philippines. While the guilt of his son Andal Ampatuan, Jr. is yet to be proved in court, the Sr. Ampatuan's complicity in the crime of the 21st century (so far) is obvious to many because the backhoe that was used to move the dirt that covered the bodies of the 57 murdered Maguindanaoans and journalists was property of Maguindanao province. It is inconceivable to many that the provincial property could have been used for the

purpose without the governor's approval.

2. The Ampatuan brothers, scions of Andal Ampatuan, Sr., who have been identified by eyewitnesses as having participated in the murder of the 57 Maguindanaoans and journalists. The brothers are a long way from being convicted of anything, of course, but then again...there are witnesses.

3. The Ayatollahs of Iran, who brutally quashed the Iranian students and freedom fighters who were agitating for electoral reforms.

4. The Pakistani-led mass murderers who went on a rampage in the streets of Bombay, India.

The Lords of Chutzpah (Filipino translation - Ang Kapal ng Mga Mukha)

1. Former Philippine President Joseph Estrada, who is running for President - again - after serving time in prison and house arrest following his conviction for the crime of plunder of the Philippine treasury.

2. The Philippine Commission on Elections, for allowing Estrada to run for President again and for its egregiously one-sided decision in the Dy vs. Padaca electoral complaint.
3. President Gloria Macapagal Arroyo and the Arroyo clan, for filing candidacies for Congress despite their dismally low approval ratings and despite questions about the legitimacy of the Arroyo presidency and the widespread allegations that the family is corrupt to the core. Also, for her decision to attend a conference in Asia while half a million Filipinos remained homeless as Typhoon Ondoy floodwaters continued to threaten their lives.

4. Former First Lady Imelda Marcos, for thinking that she deserves to be elected Congresswoman from an Ilocos Norte, Philippines district being vacated by her son, who is running for

governor of the province.

5. U.S. Senator Joseph Lieberman of Connecticut, for opposing the expansion of Medicare which he previously championed as a candidate for President in 2004, presumably as a vindictive attempt to plunge a stick in the eye of U.S. progressives.

6. Former Alaska Governor Sarah Palin, for suggesting that the health reform bill was establishing "death panels" that would decide on which old people lived, and which ones died to save government money.

7. "President" Ahmadinejad of Iran, for claiming that he won the Iranian election "fair and square."

8. Senator Panfilo Lacson of the Philippines, for fingering Estrada as the mastermind in the Bobby Dacer murder, despite the fact that everyone in the Philippines - all 90 million of them - know that Estrada's henchman during the two's glory days was none other than Panfilo Lacson.

9. Governor Mark Sanford of South Carolina and U.S. Senator John Ensign of Nevada, for refusing to resign after being exposed for marital infidelity and probable ethical misconduct in the use of public funds and in the case of Ensign, the alleged use of campaign funds to silence the husband in his adulterous menage a trois.

10. Former U.S. Vice-President Dick Cheney, for suggesting that President Obama is neglecting Afghanistan, after he and former President George Bush neglected Afghanistan from 2003 through 2008.

11. The U.S. banks that were "too big to fail," for refusing to grant small business loans after the U.S. government bailed them out from near-certain bankruptcy. Instead, the banks invested the bail-out money in the fast-recovering stock and financial instruments markets and made record profits.

The Worst Persons in the World (apologies to Keith Olbermann)

1. Glenn Beck and Rush Limbaugh of Fox News. Beck for calling African-American President Obama a racist and Limbaugh for wishing that the economy stays bad so the American people will turn on Obama and the Democrats.

2. President Gloria M. Arroyo for declaring martial law in Maguindanao, apparently to protect the Ampatuans, after doing nothing to prevent the slaughter of the Ampatuans' political enemies and independent journalists.

3. Ayatollah Khamenei, the Supreme ruler of Iran, for allowing the murder, rape and torture of Iranian electoral protesters in the aftermath of the disputed Presidential election in that country.

There you go, folks. Comments and suggestions for additional award recipients and citations are welcome.

11 - Strangers in Our Own Country

Casiano P. Mayor Jr.

Casiano P. Mayor Jr. is author of the book The Gypsy Soul and Other Essays, from which this essay was lifted with his consent. This essay was first published in the Saudi Gazette on January 25, 2003, for which he works as a journalist/editor.

Dateline, Jan. 25, 2003

Two items which appeared on this page last week prompted me to ponder about our wanderings as migrant workers. One was a photograph showing Filipino women in an employment agency seeking job placement overseas. The other was the news report about how Filipino families back home are slashing their spending on food to stretch the family budget for other basic necessities like fuel, electricity and water.

The two items underscored how difficult life has become in our country. The queue of overseas jobseekers had given flesh to the government statistics that more than 2,000 Filipinos leave the country everyday for greener pastures in some foreign lands. Those who have seen the photograph, which appeared on this page Tuesday last week, could have felt a sense of empathy with the jobseekers.

We have had our own shares of experiences similar to theirs

before we came to our new jobsites in the Kingdom. Many of us had queued outside job placement agencies in Manila or other key cities in the archipelago, braving the scorching sun and eating banana cue for lunch with high hopes that life would turn for the better when we find our dream jobs overseas.

My own family did feel the pinch of hard times before I came to Jeddah in1999. Although we had made it a point not to miss paying our electricity bills because we knew that Meralco would have cut our power line with neither pity nor compunction a few days after the bill is due, we did miss on several occasions paying our telephone bills and our monthly
amortization for our housing loan from the Social Security System.

There had been times when I felt sorry for my wife while we watched our one-year-old child enjoy her "chicken joy" at Jollibee while neither of us took anything because we could not afford to order meals for ourselves after buying our weekly groceries at SM supermarket. I felt self-pity when I had to rummage the shoe racks at Shoe Mart in 1998 hoping to find a pair of shoes for P200 or a little more – at a time when a decent pair of kids' shoes cost at least P500 – to replace a worn out pair I was wearing. I had known hard times after my father died when I was 13. I call myself a self-made man with a sense of pride, having made my way through college on my own, first as a construction laborer and then as a security guard, after I left my uncle's household in Romblon to follow my stars elsewhere. But it is different when one faces trying times alone than when he wrestles with them to fend for a family.

Alone I had slept on piles of plywood at construction jobsites with nary a care on whether I would breathe my last that night. I was living for myself with no family to worry about. But we all know that it would be different when we have families to look after. We have to feather the nest and see to it that our households have decent meals on the dinning table. Alone, we can be reckless gladiators taunting death; with our families depending on us, we become cautious knights taking the risks only when necessary.

That brings me to a dinner I had with Jun Anabo, a college classmate in Manila whom I met by chance a few months ago in a hospital where my wife and I took our child for treatment of her coughing.. We talked about life in general – life in college, our hopes when we were young and how difficult times had become back home after our economy had collapsed since the time of the late dictator Ferdinand Marcos. It was time to hark back to the days of yore when we were young journalism students who had set up our own campus newsletter because we felt that the official school publication was not serving the interest of the students but those of the school administration and Marcos's.

We belonged to a group of students who took seriously our share of social burden to help change our corrupt social and political system. It was at a time when migration to other countries, mainly to the United States, was the domain of doctors and nurses. It was a time when I felt that our doctors and nurses who migrated to the US had no sense of patriotism.

Over dinner at Shawly restaurant in Balad, we laughed at how we had lost the conviction to fight for a better country. Like most idealist students in our time, we have been gobbled by the same system we had wanted to change. The traditional politicians, whom we had despised like plagues, won and have continued to dominate the political landscape back home.

Also over dinner, Jun and I talked about migrating to other countries before Saudization catches up with us. That night we were not the young gladiators we used to be.. We were cautious old knights plotting a retreat to some foreign lands, forlorn that we had to leave our own homeland after it has been plundered by our politicians whose dreams could not go beyond basking in the glory of wealth and power.

That Tuesday night was a bitter-sweet reminder that I have long shed off any illusion that I still have a burning fervor of a patriot in me, no matter if the government keeps on telling us, overseas Filipino workers (OFWs), that we are heroes because our remittances have helped prop up our ailing economy.

I am an OFW but I am not a hero. I did not come here out of my sense of patriotism but as a husband and a father who wanted to see a new dawn for my family, no matter if that dawn unfolds in some other countries.

I have come to terms with reality. Like millions of our compatriots who had left our homeland for greener pastures in other parts of the world, I have hitched my wagon to a caravan of Filipino migrant workers who have become strangers in our own country..

12 - The Gypsy Soul

Casiano P. Mayor Jr

Casiano P. Mayor Jr. is author of the book The Gypsy Soul and Other Essays, from which this essay was lifted with his consent. This essay was first published in the Saudi Gazette, for which he works as a journalist/editor.

Dateline, Jan. 28, 1997

A letter to the editor published in the opinion page of this paper last week stabbed me in the heart. It told of the Filipino poet Federico Licsi Espino being confined at the mental hospital in Mandaluyong. The pathos of his fate lingered with me for quite a while and made me grapple on whether to write about it ifonly to let go of some strong, strange feelings that usually seize me when I am depressed. It is at times like this, when I get emotionally charged, that I itch to write. For I love to write not from the intellect but from the heart.

The day I read the letter sent by Leopoldo Ortega, I called up the poet's brother, Romeo Licsi Espino, whose name and telephone number were listed in the letter. I wanted to get his address so that I could send small amounts every now and then, when my budget permits, to help defray the expenses for Espino's treatment. He wasn't at home, but a lady who answered the phone gave me the address. I don't know the Espinos personally. I have never met the poet but I had picked up one of his books of poems – the one where he wrote about "cornflowers" – when I once rummaged the bookstores when I was still in college. I have high regards for poets since I was in high school. Although I often did not understand their poetry, I was happy to appreciate a line or two.

In the case of Espino, I have never forgotten his verse on the wind being a gypsy. Probably it is because it brings back sharp memories of Ginablan where the gypsy wind roamed freely on my aunt's corn farm on a craggy hill of San Pedro..

Espino, as the letter said, was a six-time Palanca awardee for literature, including two first prizes for poetry, aside from being first prize winner in Spain's Ramon de Basterra Memorial Awards in Spanish poetry in 1997 and the Enrique Zobel de Ayala award.

But with what befell him what good will all his awards be, for him and his family? The high cost of his treatment, it was said, has left the family impoverished. Espino's tragic fate reminds me of life's uncertainties, its emptiness, and its mysteries and of our own insignificance, no matter how we bloat our egos beyond what we really are. It raises a big question on life's meaning which probably many of us have tried to grapple with when we look beyond our daily grind..

After we have achieved what we had hoped to do when we were young, what do we gain when death – if not insanity – overtakes us? Shakespeare answered that question with his famous line about life being a "stage full of sound and fury signifying nothing." The book of Ecclesiastes in the Bible says that all our achievements are meaningless, just like "chasing the wind." Jesus Christ answered the issue with another query: "What does it profit man to gain the whole world and loses his own soul?"

My search for meaning in life introduced me to atheism when I was in college. It made me see life's emptiness in the dilemma confronted by Albert Camus's Sisyphus when he was punished by the mythical gods to roll a boulder up a hill and back each time the boulder rolls down as soon as he reaches the top. It lured me into the world of Marx and I almost did follow him but for my reservation about his theory to create a "classless society," which I thought was a utopia. I was more at home with the existentialists and, in the later part of my college days, had even prepared an epithet for my tomb, "Here lays the body of a man who never knew who he was and why he lived."

But if life's emptiness and uncertainties made me stray to atheism, they also drove me back to my old religion, Christianity. In my wanderings since I left Romblon, I have come to realize that man has a soul longing for a home. His soul made Espino a gypsy like the wind wandering in his poetry. German philosopher Friedrich Nietzsche, although an atheist, was no exception. He was a gypsy soul.

Our soul has kept on driving us in search for meaning, whether we live in a craggy hill of some remote villages or in the jungles of modern sky crappers in some mega cities, probably to remind us that we are but pilgrims in this world longing for home.

13 - An End To Cheating
Sonny B. Coloma, PhD

*Courtesy and permission of **Sonny Coloma** and his blogsite,
http://sonnycoloma.blogspot.com   Prof. Coloma is the Don Jose
Cojuangco Professor of Business Mgt at Asian Institute of Management
or AIM. He served under President Cory Aquino and President Joseph
Estrada in various high postions. He was consultant to the Senate and
the House. He became President of University of Makati from 1996-99.
He was a VP at Far East Bank. He is acive in the Rotary and he
received various commendations as a civic leader. He finished college
in UP'73, earned MA at AIM and PhD at Southast Asia Interdisciplinary
Develpment Institute or SAIDI.*

Dateline, Sunday, November 1, 2009

"A lot of people can cheat. They cheat by just a little bit. When
we remind people about their morality, they cheat less. When we
get bigger distance from cheating, from the object of money, for
example, people cheat more. And when we see cheating around
us, particularly if it's part of our own in-group, cheating goes up."

Dan Ariely, a professor of behavioral economics at Duke

University, came up worth the foregoing conclusions after conducting several experiments to validate certain intuitive assumptions about the way people behave.

In the aftermath of the deluge brought about by typhoons *Ondoy* and *Pepeng*, there's been a lot of reflective thinking on what went wrong. Particularly instructive was a statement made by a friend, Felino (Jun) Palafox, an architect and urban planner, that the massive destruction was "not an act of God", but an offshoot of an accumulation of human sins of omission and commission, especially those against the environment.

Indeed, a lot of people cheated. They cheated on the environment by constructing houses in areas already known to be danger or threat zones on account of being a water basin, as in the Marikina disaster. They cheated by cutting trees indiscriminately dumping their garbage mindlessly.

So what made them behave that way? Prof. Ariely's experiments tell us a lot. (Readers may see the website: *http://www.TED.com*)

For example, when offered money in return for being able to recall the Ten Commandments from memory, they were more honest than when they were asked to declare how many questions in an economics quiz did they get right. Hence, Prof. Ariely concludes that people cheat less when they are reminded about morality.

When an actor was planted in a group that was being tested for honesty, the group readily followed the cheating initiated by the actor when he was wearing the sweatshirt of their own school. But, in another experiment, they did not follow a planted actor who was wearing the sweatshirt of their archrival school. They were more honest because they did not want to act in a way that was associated with an organization that they did not want to be identified with.

This latter experiment is what prompts him to hypothesize that "when we see cheating around us, particularly with our own in-group, cheating goes up."

Being a behavioral economist, his focus was on trying to explain what went wrong with Wall Street. So he reflects: "What happens in a situation when you pay people lots of money to see reality in a slightly distorted way? What if, instead of money, you offered them stocks, stock options, derivatives and mortgage-backed securities? Could it be that with these more distant things, it's something many steps removed from money for a much longer time, could it be that people would cheat even more?"

With these series of rhetorical questions, he offers an explanation for the reign of greed that brought Wall Street down late last year. Then he asks, "What happens to the social environment when people see other people behave around them in certain ways?" That's a question we need to ask ourselves in our efforts to discern what it will take to bring about meaningful change in our country.

What do these findings imply for us Filipinos?

First, we need to be reminded about morality. Who can remind us in a way that will influence us to act morally, ethically or honestly? Only a credible leader who walks the talk; one who is perceived to be clearly good, ethical and moral. President Corazon Aquino was such a sterling role model. Hence, her legacy is that of faithful stewardship and good governance. Almost two decades after she stepped down from power, the Filipino people expressed their affection for her by braving rain and fatigue during her funeral procession.

Second, when a culture of cheating predominates, people tend to look the other way and would even be in denial of the reality, until they are jolted out of their indifference or complacency. This is what happened during all these years of the Arroyo presidency, particularly after the 'Hello Garci' scandal.

Many people lapsed into a state of denial, allowing themselves to be deluded into adopting a defeatist mindset expressed in the query, "*Eh, sino ba ang ipapalit ninyo*" ("So whom you will tap to replace her?). This was after they realized that the constitutional successor, Vice President Noli de Castro did not really offer the prospect of being a significantly better President.

This seeming lack of a sense of outrage among our citizenry prompted administration lackeys to run roughshod and throw out impeachment resolutions filed against the President. Using their superior numbers to steamroller the opposition, they have also mounted an attempt to change the constitution through the constituent assembly route after the Supreme Court previously ruled against the people's initiative mode of charter change.

And then came the fateful events of August. A sea of yellow emerged and brought forth a fresh wave of optimism that yes, the spirit of *Edsa Uno* is still alive. And just as the final cast of characters for the 2010 presidential derby was shaping up came the deluge. The floods could not wash all the sins of the past away.

As an old song goes, "The answer, my friends, is blowing in the wind." The winds of change are upon us.
We want honest government. We want a leader who will remind us that we can be good when we want to be good, that goodness is what will make our lives better. We need a leader we can believe in, a leader who can make us believe in our capacity for change. (sonnycoloma@gmail.com)

14 - Toward A Culture of Giving, Not Having

Sonny B. Coloma, PhD

Courtesy and permission of Sonny Coloma and his blogsite, http://sonnycoloma.blogspot.com Prof. Coloma is the Don Jose Cojuangco Professor of Business Mgt. at Asian Institute of Management or AIM. He served under President Cory Aquino and President Joseph Estrada in various high postions. He was consultant to the Senate and the House. He became President of University of Makati from 1996-99. He was a VP at Far East Bank. He is acive in the Rotary and he received various commendations as a civic leader. He finished college in UP'73, earned MA at AIM and PhD at Southast Asia Interdisciplinary Develpment Institute or SAIDI.

Dateline, Sunday, November 1, 2009

Whenever the idea of increasing the minimum wage is raised, the captains of Philippine industry are first to oppose and object. They raise the specter of widespread loss of jobs and paint scenarios of gloom and doom. No wonder then that when a bill was proposed in Congress many years ago to require owners of private corporations to share profits with their employees, they also registered their vigorous objection.

Compared with neighboring ASEAN countries, the Philippines has one of the worst income distribution patterns in this region. Nowhere else is it more true that in this blighted land, only the rich become richer and the poor get even poorer. Paradoxically, the Philippines is also the only Christian country in Southeast Asia, with nearly 90% of its citizens being baptized Roman Catholics.

From Chiara Lubich's perspective, the Philippines is not just a Third World country in the sense of being materially underdeveloped. In the book, *Essential Writings*, the founder of the Focolare movement shares her thoughts on spirituality, dialogue and culture. She also calls attention to the fact that we are also "underdeveloped Christians" because we fail to live up to God's commandment that we "love him with all one's heart, mind, and strength".

She says that according to Catherine of Siena and Teresa of Avila, both doctors of the Church, and Thomas Aquinas and Francis de Sales, "only those who have reached the full development of love could call themselves real Christians, Christians who are, so to speak, 'actualized'."

She raises the bar even further when she points out that "this conviction corresponds to the often little-understood words of the Master directed to everyone: 'Be perfect, therefore, as your heavenly Father is perfect' (Matthew 5:48)".

If Chiara Lubich were to mount a public podium today and talk about the Focolare movement's concept of The Economy of Communion (EOC), she would be a most effective advocate of an alternative to a decadent and bankrupt global economic system.

Writing on *Spirituality and the Economy of Communion Businesses*, Lorna Gold outlined the key precept on sharing of profits that underpins the Focolare philosophy:

"The idea of businesses making profits and sharing them in three parts...was laden with assumptions about the nature of profits, and as a consequence, the way profits ought to be made."

Since the heart of the Focolare revolves around the creation of spaces in which there are relationships founded on love – 'Trinitarian relationships' – the businesses has to reflect this spirit in everything that they did. Profits, therefore, could not be the result of efficiency savings borne out of exploitation, coercion or corruption – they had to be the result of a new relationship above all between the people within the businesses. The start of the EOC, therefore, also regarded the nature of the individual businesses themselves and the way that their profits were made.

According to the Trinitarian concept embedded in the philosophy of the Focolare's Economy of Communion, the wealth (or profits) created by the enterprise is to be shared in three ways: a) reinvestment in the company; b) distribution to the poor and those in need; and c) to the community, by way of infrastructure that will promote the culture of giving --- model towns, publishing houses, formation centers.

In Essential Writings, which will be launched this weekend in Manila, Ms. Lubich emphasizes four points about the Economy of Communion: first, its aim or purpose; second, the "culture of giving" which is its hallmark; third, the "new men and women" who are mainly instrumental for managing this new economy; and fourth, the "schools of formation" that must be instituted for these same men and women.

She explains: "The aim of the Economy of Communion is hidden within its very name: it is an economy that has to do with communion among people and sharing of goods...Its aim...is to work toward unity and fraternity among the whole human family according to Jesus' prayer to the Father: 'May all be one', to the point of becoming one heart and one soul through mutual charity." Hence, the Focolare movement espouses among its members a "spirituality of unity."

The culture of giving is "the antidote to the culture of having so dominant today"; in fact, it is this culture of unbridled grid that has spawned and accelerated the present global economic crisis. Such culture of giving is also a culture of love, says Ms. Lubich, "because the human person made in the image of God who is love, finds fulfillment precisely in loving, in giving."

Her concept of loving and giving is quite pervasive as she points out that the Economy of Communion "does not ask us to love only the needy, but everyone." Thus, she issues this clarion call: ("The EOC") asks that we love all those who in one way or another are involved in the business."

What does this mean in practical terms? She describes how this is to be done: "Let's give always: give a smile, understanding, forgiveness, our listening; let's give our intelligence, our will and our availability; let's give our experience and skills. Give: let this be the word that gives us no rest."

Specifically addressing men and women who hold positions of responsibility in the business sector, she quotes from St. Thomas Aquinas: "When for their personal benefit the rich consume the surplus necessary for the sustenance of the poor, they steal from them." Then she states affirmatively: "A bit of charity, a few works of mercy, a small amount of surplus from individuals is not enough (to reach our goal); entire companies and businesses must freely put in common their profits."

Will Ms. Lubich's emphatic statements find resonance among the leaders of Philippine business? I don't think so. Yet, I believe Ms. Lubich's message needs to be proclaimed with urgency at this time of economic turmoil. A paradigm shift is clearly needed. Business leaders must begin viewing the real world with a new set of lenses.

Comments are welcome at sonnycoloma@gmail.com

15 - Reasons to be Proud Pinoys (Satire)

Anonymous

FROM the 1896 Revolution to the first Philippine Republic, the Commonwealth period, the EDSA Revolt, and the tiger cub economy, history marches on. Thankfully, however, some things never change. Like the classics, things irresistibly Pinoy mark us for life. They're the indelible stamp of our identity, the undeniable affinity that binds us like twins. They celebrate the good in us, the best of our culture and the infinite possibilities we are all capable of. Some are so self-explanatory you only need mention them for fellow Pinoys to swoon or drool. Here, from all over this Centennial-crazed country and in no particular order, are a hundred of the best things that make us unmistakably Pinoy. (Thanks to the author for circulating this freely in cyberspace)

Merienda. Where else is it normal to eat five times a day?

Sawsawan. Assorted sauces that guarantee freedom of choice, enough room for experimentation and maximum tolerance for diverse tastes. Favorites: toyo't calamansi, suka at sili, patis.

Kuwan, ano. At a loss for words? Try these and marvel at how Pinoys understand exactly what you want.

Pinoy humor and irreverence. If you're api and you know it, crack a joke. Nothing personal, really.

Tingi. Thank goodness for small entrepreneurs. Where else can we buy cigarettes, soap, condiments and life's essentials in small affordable amounts?

Spirituality. Even before the Spaniards came, ethnic tribes had their own anitos, bathalas and assorted deities, pointing to a strong relationship with the Creator, who or whatever it may be.

Po, opo, mano po. Speech suffixes that define courtesy, deference, filial respect--a balm to the spirit in these aggressive times.

Pasalubong. Our way of sharing the vicarious thrills and delights of a trip, and a wonderful excuse to shop without the customary guilt.

Beaches! With 7,000 plus islands, we have miles and miles of shoreline piled high with fine white sand, lapped by warm waters, and nibbled by exotic tropical fish. From the stormy seas of Batanes to the emerald isles of Palawan--over here, life is truly a beach.

Bagoong. Darkly mysterious, this smelly fish or shrimp paste typifies the underlying theme of most ethnic foods: disgustingly unhygienic, unbearably stinky and simply irresistible.

Bayanihan. Yes, the internationally-renowned dance company, but also this habit of pitching in still common in small communities. Just have that cold beer and some pulutan ready for the troops.

The Balikbayan box. Another way of sharing life's bounty, no matter if it seems like we're fleeing Pol Pot every time we head home from anywhere in the globe. The most wonderful part is that, more often than not, the contents are carted home to be distributed.

Pilipino komiks. Not to mention "Hiwaga," "Aliwan," "Tagalog Classics," "Liwayway" and"Bulaklak" magazines. Pulpy publications that gave us Darna, Facifica Falayfay, Lagalag, Kulafu, Kenkoy, Dyesebel, characters of a time both innocent and worldly.

Folk songs. They come unbidden and spring, full blown, like a second language, at the slightest nudge from the too-loud stereo of a passing jeepney or tricycle.

Fiesta. Eat, drink and be merry, for tomorrow is just another day, shrugs the poor man who, once a year, honors a patron saint with this sumptuous, no-holds-barred spread. It's a Pinoy celebration at its pious and riotous best.

Aswang, manananggal, kapre. The whole underworld of Filipino lower mythology recalls our uniquely bizarre childhood, that is, before political correctness kicked in. Still, their rich adventures pepper our storytelling.

Jeepneys. Colorful, fast, reckless, a vehicle of postwar Pinoy ingenuity, this Everyman's communal cadillac makes for a cheap, interesting ride. If the driver's a daredevil (as they usually are), hang on to your seat.

Dinuguan. Blood stew, a bloodcurdling idea, until you try it with puto. Best when mined with jalapeño peppers. Messy but delicious.

Santacruzan. More than just a beauty contest, this one has religious overtones, a tableau of St. Helena's and Constantine's search for the Cross that seamlessly blends piety, pageantry and ritual. Plus, it's the perfect excuse to show off the prettiest ladies--and the most beautiful gowns.

Balut. Unhatched duck's embryo, another unspeakable ethnic food to outsiders, but oh, to indulge in guilty pleasures! Sprinkle some salt and suck out that soup, with gusto.

Pakidala. A personalized door-to-door remittance and delivery system for overseas Filipino workers who don't trust the banking system, and who expect a family update from the courier, as well.

Choc-nut. Crumbly peanut chocolate bars that defined childhood ecstasy before M & M's and Hershey's.

Kamayan style. To eat with one's hand and eschew spoon, fork and table manners--ah, heaven.

Chicharon. Pork, fish or chicken crackling. There is in the crunch a hint of the extravagant, the decadent and the pedestrian. Perfect with vinegar, sublime with beer.

Pinoy hospitality. Just about everyone gets a hearty "Kain tayo!" invitation to break bread with whoever has food to share, no matter how skimpy or austere it is.

Adobo, kare-kare, sinigang and other lutong bahay stuff. Home-cooked meals that have the stamp of approval from several generations, who swear by closely-guarded cooking secrets and family recipes.

Lola Basyang. The voice one heard spinning tales over the radio, before movies and television curtailed imagination and defined grown-up tastes.

Pambahay. Home is where one can let it all hang out, where clothes do not make a man or woman but rather define their level of comfort.

Tricycle and trisikad, the poor Pinoy's taxicab that delivers you at your doorstep for as little as PHPesos3.00, with a complimentary dusting of polluted air.

Dirty ice cream. Very Pinoy flavors that make up for the risk: munggo, langka, ube, mais, keso, macapuno. Plus there's the colorful cart that recalls jeepney art.

Yayas. The trusted Filipino nanny who, ironically, has become a major Philippine export as overseas contract workers. A good one is almost like a surrogate parent--if you don't mind the accent and the predilection for afternoon soap and movie stars.

Sarsi. Pinoy rootbeer, the enduring taste of childhood. Our grandfathers had them with an egg beaten in.

Pinoy fruits. Atis, guyabano, chesa, mabolo, lanzones, durian, langka, makopa, dalanghita, siniguelas, suha, chico, papaya, singkamas--the possibilities!

Filipino celebrities. Movie stars, broadcasters, beauty queens, public officials, all-around controversial figures: Aurora Pijuan, Cardinal Sin, Carlos P. Romulo, Charito Solis, Cory Aquino, Emilio Aguinaldo, the Eraserheads, Fidel V. Ramos, Francis Magalona, Gloria Diaz, Manuel L. Quezon, Margie Moran, Melanie Marquez, Ninoy Aquino, Nora Aunor, Pitoy Moreno, Ramon Magsysay, Richard Gomez, San Lorenzo Ruiz, Sharon Cuneta, Gemma Cruz, Erap,Tiya Dely,Mel andJay,Gary V.

World class Pinoys who put us on the global map: Lea Salonga, Paeng Nepomuceno, Eugene Torre, Luisito Espinosa, Lydia de Vega-Mercado, Jocelyn Enriquez, Elma Muros, Onyok Velasco, Efren "Bata" Reyes, Lilia Calderon-Clemente, Loida Nicolas-Lewis, Josie Natori.

Pinoy tastes. A dietitian's nightmare: too sweet, too salty, too fatty, as in burong talangka, itlog na maalat, crab fat (aligue), bokayo, kutchinta, sapin-sapin, halo-halo, pastilyas, palitaw, pulburon, longganisa, tuyo, ensaymada, ube haleya, sweetened macapuno and garbanzos. Remember, we're the guys who put sugar (horrors) in our spaghetti sauce. Yum!

The sights. Banaue Rice Terraces, Boracay, Bohol's Chocolate Hills, Corregidor Island, Fort Santiago, the Hundred Islands, the Las Pi?s **Bamboo Organ**, Rizal Park, Mt. Banahaw, Mayon Volcano, Taal Volcano. A land of contrasts and ever-changing landscapes.

Gayuma, agimat and anting-anting. Love potions and amulets. How the socially-disadvantaged Pinoy copes.

Barangay, Ginebra, Jaworski, PBA, MBA and basketball. How the verticaly-challenged Pinoy compensates, via a national sports obsession that reduces fans to tears and fistfights.

People Power at EDSA. When everyone became a hero and changed Philippine history overnight.

San Miguel Beer and pulutan. "Isa pa nga!" and the Philippines' most popular, world-renowned beer goes well with peanuts, corniks, tapa, chicharon, usa, barbecue, sisig, and all manner of spicy, crunchy and cholesterol-rich chasers.

Resiliency. We've survived 400 years of Spanish rule, the US bases, Marcos, the 1990 earthquake, lahar, lambada, Robin Padilla, and Tamagochi. We'll survive Erap.

Yoyo. Truly Filipino in origin, this hunting tool, weapon, toy and merchandising vehicle remains the best way to "walk the dog" and "rock the baby," using just a piece of string.

Pinoy games: Pabitin, palosebo, basagan ng palayok. A few basic rules make individual cunning and persistence a premium, and guarantee a good time for all.

Ninoy Aquino. For saying that "the Filipino is worth dying for," and proving it.

Balagtasan. The verbal joust that brings out rhyme, reason and passion on a public stage.

Tabo. All-powerful, ever-useful, hygienically-triumphant device to scoop water out of a bucket _ and help the true Pinoy answer nature's call. Helps maintain our famously stringent toilet habits.

Pandesal. Despite its shrinking size, still a good buy. Goes well with any filling, best when hot.

Jollibee. Truly Pinoy in taste and sensibility, and a corporate icon that we can be quite proud of. Do you know that it's invaded the Middle East, as well?

The butanding, the dolphins and other creatures in our blessed waters. They're Pinoys, too, and they're here to stay. Now if some folks would just stop turning them into daing.

Pakikisama. It's what makes people stay longer at parties, have another drink, join pals in sickness and health. You can get dead drunk and still make it home.

Sing-a-long. Filipinos love to sing, and thank God a lot of us do it well!

Kayumanggi. Neither pale nor dark, our skin tone is beautifully healthy, the color of a rich earth or a mahogany tree growing towards the sun.

Handwoven cloth and native weaves. Colorful, environment-friendly alternatives to polyester that feature skillful workmanship and a rich indigenous culture behind every thread. From the pinukpok of the north to the malong of the south, it's the fiber of who we are.

Movies. Still the cheapest form of entertainment, especially if you watch the same movie several times.

Bahala na. We cope with uncertainty by embracing it, and are thus enabled to play life by ear.

Papaitan. An offal stew flavored with bile, admittedly an acquired taste, but pointing to our national ability to acquire a taste for almost anything.

English. Whether carabao or Arr-neoww-accented, it doubles our chances in the global marketplace.

The Press. Irresponsible, sensational, often inaccurate, but still the liveliest in Asia. Otherwise, we'd all be glued to TV.

Divisoria. Smelly, crowded, a pickpocket's paradise, but you can get anything here, often at rock-bottom prices. The sensory overload is a bonus.

Barong Tagalog. Enables men to look formal and dignified without having to strangle themselves with a necktie. Worn well, it makes any ordinary Juan look marvelously makisig.

Filipinas. They make the best friends, lovers, wives. Too bad they can't say the same for Filipinos.

Filipinos. So maybe they're bolero and macho with an occasional streak of generic infidelity; they do know how to make a woman feel like one.

Catholicism. What fun would sin be without guilt? Jesus Christ is firmly planted on Philippine soil.

Dolphy. Our favorite, ultra-durable comedian gives the beleaguered Pinoy everyman an odd dignity, even in drag.

Style. Something we often prefer over substance. But every Filipino claims it as a birthright.

Bad taste. Clear plastic covers on the vinyl-upholstered sofa, posters of poker-playing dogs masquerading as art, overaccessorized jeepneys and altars--the list is endless, and wealth only seems to magnify it.

Mangoes. Crisp and tart, or lusciously ripe, they evoke memories of family outings and endless sunshine in a heart-shaped package.Mangoes. Crisp and tart, or lusciously ripe, they evoke memories of family outings and endless sunshine in a heart-shaped package.

Unbridled optimism. Why we rank so low on the suicide scale.

Street food: Barbecue, lugaw, banana-cue, fishballs, IUD (chicken entrails), adidas (chicken feet), warm taho. Forget hepatitis; here's cheap, tasty food with gritty ambience.

The siesta. Snoozing in the middle of the day is smart, not lazy.

Honorifics and courteous titles: Kuya, ate, diko, ditse, ineng, totoy, Ingkong, Aling, Mang, etc. No exact English translation, but these words connote respect, deference and the value placed on kinship.

Heroes and people who stood up for truth and freedom. Lapu-lapu started it all, and other heroes and revolutionaries followed: Diego Silang, Macario Sakay, Jose Rizal, Andres Bonifacio, Apolinario Mabini, Melchora Aquino, Gregorio del Pilar, Gabriela Silang, Miguel Malvar, Francisco Balagtas, Juan Luna, Marcelo H. del Pilar, Panday Pira, Emilio Jacinto, Raha Suliman, Antonio Luna, Gomburza, Emilio Aguinaldo, the heroes of Bataan and Corregidor, Pepe Diokno, Satur Ocampo, Dean Armando Malay, Evelio Javier, Ninoy Aquino, Lola Rosa and other comfort women who spoke up, honest cabbie Emilio Advincula, Rona Mahilum, the women lawyers who didn't let Jalosjos get away with rape.

Flora and fauna. The sea cow (dugong), the tarsier, calamian deer, bearcat, Philippine eagle, sampaguita, ilang-ilang, camia, pandan, the creatures that make our archipelago unique.

Pilipino songs, OPM and composers: "Ama Namin," "Lupang Hinirang," "Gaano Ko Ikaw Kamahal," "Ngayon at Kailanman," "Anak," "Handog,""Hindi Kita Malilimutan," "Ang Pasko ay Sumapit"; Ryan Cayabyab, George Canseco, Restie Umali, Levi Celerio, Manuel Francisco, Freddie Aguilar, and Florante--living examples of our musical gift.

Metro Aides. They started out as Imelda Marcos' groupies, but have gallantly proven their worth. Against all odds, they continuously prove that cleanliness is next to godliness--especially now that those darned candidates' posters have to be scraped off the face of Manila!

Sari-sari store. There's one in every corner, offering everything from bananas and floor wax to Band-Aid and bakya.

Philippine National Red Cross. PAWS. Caritas. Fund drives. They help us help each other.

Favorite TV shows through the years: "Tawag ng Tanghalan," "John and Marsha," "Champoy," "Ryan, Ryan Musikahan," "Kuwarta o Kahon," "Public Forum/Lives," "Student Canteen," "Eat Bulaga." In the age of inane variety shows, they have redeemed Philippine television.

Quirks of language that can drive crazy any tourist listening in: "Bababa ba?" "Bababa!"

"Sayang!" "Naman!" "Kadiri!" "Ano ba!?" "pala." Expressions that defy translation but wring out feelings genuinely Pinoy.

Cockfighting. Filipino men love it more than their wives (sometimes).

Dr. Jose Rizal. A category in himself. Hero, medicine man, genius, athlete, sculptor, fictionist, poet, essayist, husband, lover, samaritan, martyr. Truly someone to emulate and be proud of, anytime, anywhere.

Nora Aunor. Short, dark and homely-looking, she redefined our rigid concept of how leading ladies should look.

Noranian or Vilmanian. Defines the friendly rivalry between Ate Guy Aunor and Ate Vi Santos and for many years, the only way to be for many Filipino fans.

Filipino Christmas. The world's longest holiday season. A perfect excuse to mix our love for feasting, gift-giving and music and wrap it up with a touch of religion.

Relatives and kababayan abroad. The best refuge against loneliness, discrimination and confusion in a foreign place. Distant relatives and fellow Pinoys readily roll out the welcome mat even on the basis of a phone introduction or referral.

Festivals: Sinulog, Ati-atihan, Moriones. Sounds, colors, pagan frenzy and Christian overtones.

Folk dances. Tinikling, pandanggo sa ilaw, kari?sa, kuratsa, itik-itik, alitaptap, rigodon. All the right moves and a distinct rhythm.

Native wear and costumes. Baro't saya, tapis, terno, saya, salakot, bakya. Lovely form and ingenious function in the way we dress.

Sunday family gatherings. Or, close family ties that never get severed. You don't have to win the lotto or be a president to have 10,000 relatives. Everyone's family tree extends all over the archipelago, and it's at its best in times of crisis; notice how food, hostesses, money, and moral support materialize during a wake?

Calesa and karitela. The colorful and leisurely way to negotiate narrow streets when loaded down with a year's provisions.

Quality of life. Where else can an ordinary employee afford a stay-in helper, a yaya, unlimited movies, eat-all-you-can buffets, the latest fashion (Baclaran nga lang), even Viagra in the black market?

All Saints' Day. In honoring our dead, we also prove that we know how to live.

Handicrafts. Shellcraft, rattancraft, abaca novelties, woodcarvings, banig placemats and bags, bamboo windchimes, etc. Portable memories of home. Hindi lang pang-turista, pang-balikbayan pa!

Pinoy greens. Sitaw. Okra. Ampalaya. Gabi. Munggo. Dahon ng Sili. Kangkong. Luya. Talong. Sigarillas. Bataw. Patani. Lutong bahay will never be the same without them.

OFWs. The lengths (and miles) we'd go for a better life for our family, as proven by these modern-day heroes of the economy.

The Filipino artist. From Luna's magnificent "Spoliarium" and Amorsolo's sun-kissed ricefields, to Ang Kiukok's jarring abstractions and Borlongan's haunting ghosts, and everybody else in between. Hang a Filipino painting on your wall, and you're hanging one of Asia's best.

Tagalog soap operas. From "Gulong ng Palad" and "Flor de Luna" to today's incarnations like "Mula sa Puso"--they're the story of our lives, and we feel strongly for them, MariMar notwithstanding.

Midnight madness, weekends sales, bangketas and baratillos. It's retail therapy at its best, with Filipinos braving traffic, crowds, and human deluge to find a bargain.

Contact: job_elizes@yahoo.com - tatay@usa.com - **Listed Books:**

Writings 1 Book, 2012 + + 1. Obit, *Bambi Harper* + + **2. Speech, UP, 2003,** *Butch Jimenez* + + **3. Speech, Silliman U, 2006,** *Butch Jimenez* + + **4. The Mission Moment,** *Dr. Phil Stack* + + 5. **Subanon Spirits of Rice & Land** - *Noel Cornel Alegre* + + **6. I Look Out The Window** - *Atty. Toto Causing* + + **7. Ride On A Bus, Poem,** *Melanie Ferrer, et al* + + **8. Why Am I Doing This,** *Susie Barbieri* + **9. How To Court A Philippine Lady,** *Rodel Ramos, et al* + + **10. Story of Bacna Surgical Mission,** *Sylvia Salvador* + **11. Catch That Story,** *Tatay Jobo Elizes*

Writings 2 Book, 2012 + + 1. There Is Hope For The Philippines, *Grace Padaca* + + **2. Pointers On Employment Abroad,** *Melanie Aquino* + + **3. Without KNCHS: (Love story),** *Atty. Toto Causing* + + **4. 422 Years Ago,** *Rodel Rodis* + + **5. Filipino American History Month,** *Rodel Rodis* + + **6. A Need For Reflection, Gloom,** *Cesar Torres* + + **7. Did Ninoy Die For Nothing,** *Joey Concepcion* + + **8. Criteria - American Institute of Philanthropy,** *Charity Guidelines (Feature)* + + **9. Coming Revolution In The Ballot,** *Cesar Lumba* + + **10. 2009, A Retrospective,** *Cesar Lumba* + + **11. Strangers In Our Own Country,** *Casiano Mayor Jr.* + + **12. The Gypsy Soul,** *Casiano Mayor Jr.* + + **13. An End To Cheating,** *Sonny Coloma* + + **14. Toward Culture of Giving, Not Having,** *Sonny Coloma* + + **15. 100 Reasons to be Proud as Pinoys,** *Anonymous*

Writings 3 Book, 2010 + + I. EPIC25, Emerging Philippines Investors Coalition, *Norman Madrid* + + **II. Management Ability As An Issue,** *Dr. Rene B. Azurin* + + **III. Do We Really Want To Give Our Politicos More Power,** *Dr. Rene B. Azurin* + + **IV. Will 2010 Fulfill High Hopes For Better Life,** *Ernie D. Delfin* + + **V. Comelec Is The Root Of All Evils,** *Toto Causing* + + **VI. Advantages of Federalism/Parliamentary,** *Dr. Jose Abueva* + + **VII. Sometimes A Great Nation,** *Mar-Vic Cagurangan* + + **VIII. Great Conspiracy,** *Mar-Vic Cagurangan* + + **IX. Of Speech & Life's Riddles,** *Casiano Mayor* + + **X. Bad Start To The Year,** *Rod Garcia* + + **XI. A Dinner Out,** *Rod Garcia* + + **XII. One More Time,** *Roy Gaane* + + **XIII. Musings,** *Ceres Busa* + + **XIV. Value Formation For Good Citizenship,** *Roger Reyes, JMC Nepomuceno, Ramon Gonzales, CDVictory, Mila Marzon* + + **XV. On Being Filipino American,** *John Reyes* + + **XVI. The Monterey Peninsula,** *John Reyes* + + **XVII. The Salaza Fiesta,** *John Reyes* + + **XVIII. Salawikain: Filipino Proverbs,** *John Reyes* + + **XIX. Musikero (The Musician),** *John Reyes* + + **XX. Strange Noises,** *Tatay Jobo Elizes*

Writings 4 Book, 2010 + + I. The State of Our Nation and Democracy In 2010: Building 'The Good Society" We Want, *Dr. Jose V. Abueva* + + **II. Assessing Expanded Role of AFP in Nation Building,** *Col.Dennis Acop, Ret.* + + **III. Assessing RP's Security Strategies Alternative Views,** *Col. Dennis Acop, Ret.* + + **IV. The Way We Were,** *Fred Natividad* + + V. **Veterans of Ipo Dam, A Fiction,** *Fred Natividad* + + **VI. A Plea,** *Miguel Reyes Reynaldo* + + **VII. Int'l Youth Bowling, My Impressions,** *Marjorie Ann Elizes Reyes* + + **VIII. Mi Ultimo Adios (My Last Farewell),** *Dr. Jose P. Rizal* + + **IX. Aling Pagibig Sa Tinubuang Bayan,** *Gat. Andres Bonifacio* + + **X. Rekonsilasyun Dula (Reunion in Heaven),** *A Play, Irineo P. Goce (KaPule2 or Leonidas P. Agbayani)* + + **XI. Forgery of Rizal Retraction,** *Irineo P. Goce (KaPule2 or Leonidas P. Agbayani)* + + **XII. Maikling Kasaysayan Ng Malas Na Bayang Pilipinas,** *Ireneo P. Goce (KaPule2 or Leonidas P. Agbayani)*

Writings 5 Book - "Best Hopes" 2010, About President P-Noy + + I. The Challenge of a Hundred Days: Believing that Filipinos can, *Tony Meloto* + + II. The 2006 Ramon Magsaysay Award for Community Service, *for Tony Meloto* + + III. Open Letter to Noynoy, *F. Sionil Jose* + + IV. A History of Pain, *Juan L. Mercado* + + V. An Open Letter to Noynoy, *From OFWS* + + VI. Pursuit of Good Governance Advocacies, *Marcelo Tecson* + + VII. A Fervent Prayer for Peace, *Cesar Torres* + + VIII. A History of Betrayal, *Perry Diaz* + + IX. Corona's Thorny Crown, *Perry Diaz* + + X. Dawn of a New Era, *Perry Diaz* + + XI. Of Mice, Boys and Men, *Philip S. Chua, MD* + + XII. A Hopeful Tomorrow - A Balikbayan Insight, *Philip S. Chua, MD* + + XIII. Global Filipinos: A Sleeping Giant, *Philip S. Chua, MD* + + XIV. Heart to Heart - Winds of Change, *Philip S. Chua, MD* + + XV. Growing Old is a Privilege, *Philip S. Chua, MD* + + XVI. Our Cruelty to Mother Earth, *Philip S. Chua, MD* + + XVII. Advice to Grads: "Never Choose Your Heroes Lightly", *Ernie Delfin* + + XVIII. Gawad Kalinga, A Progressive Movement, *Ernie Delfin* + + XIX. Why a Man Must Save and Invest, *Ernie Delfin* + + XX. Beautiful San Francisco, Pinoy Heaven, *Ted Laguatan* + + XXI. The next President and PAMUSA, *Frank Wenceslao* + + XXII. Philippne Budget Deficit, *Frank Wenceslao* + + XXIII. Money Laundering: US Tools vs. Corruption, *Frank Wenceslao* + + XXIV. Amid the Fighting, Clan Rules Maguindanao, *Jaileen F. Jimeno* + + XXV. Why I Publish Writings, *Tatay Jobo Elizes*

Writings 6 Book, 2010 + + I. SONA, State Of Nation Address, English, *Pres. Benigno Aquino III* + + II. SONA, State of Nation Address, Pilipino, *Pres. Benigno Aquino III* + + III. First 100 Days Speech, Pilipino, *Pres. Benigno Aquino III* + + IV. Finally, Another Ramon Magsaysay In The Making, *Bert Guiang.* + + V. A Covenant With Our President, *Tony Meloto* + + VI. From A Grateful Heart, A Thank You Letter, *Tony Meloto* + + VII. The Scent of Hope For The Global Filipino, *Tony Meloto* + + VIII. Fleshing Out The Broad Strokes, *Felicito (Tong) C. Payumo* + + IX. In Search Of Leaders (Part1), *Felicito (Tong) C. Payumo* + + X. In Search of Leaders (Part 2), *Felicito (Tong) C. Payumo* + + XI. A Conspiracy of Dunces, *Cesar Lumba* + + XII. Only Science Can Solve Poverty, *Flor Lacanilao* + + XIII. Education Reform Amid Scarcity, *Flor Lacanilao* + + XIV. Highblood: Obituaries/Reasons, *Flor Lacanilao* + + XV. How Money Works, *Edmund Lao* + XVI. State of Economy & Society, 2002, *Juan Dela Cruz (Txtmania)* + + XVII. Global Filipinos, *Juan Dela Cruz (Txtmania)* + + XVIII. Understanding Poverty, *Juan Dla Cruz (Txtmania)* + + XIX. Kuyakuy, *Dr. Ramon Marquez* + + XX. Cambodian Octopus, *Joey Jamito* + + XXI. Inspite Of Herself, I Still Love The Philippines, *Joey Jamito* + + XXII. Love Has Wings, *Percy Campoamor Cruz* + + XXIII. Walk For Kris, *Rod Garcia* + + XXIV. Coldblooded, But Alive, *Rod Garcia* + + XXV. It Takes A Village, *Rod Garcia* + + XXVI. Beauty Contest, *Rod Garcia* + + XXVII. Eight Points In Enlightening The Elites, *Orion Perez Dumdum* + + XXVIII. Case Against "Cellphone Revolution", *Sarah Raymundo*

Writings 7 Book, 2010 - My Vintage Pics (Biographical) Tatay Jobo Elizes

Writings 8 Book, 2010 + + I. The Church and the State: In Search of Common Ground, *Gel Santos Relos* + + II. President Aquino: "Walang Kaibigan, Walang Kamag-anak", *Gel Santos Relos* + + III. What Makes Us "Pinoy", *Gel Santos Relos* + + IV. Minsan May Isang Puta (2007), *Mike Portes* + + V. Build Our Dream, *Jose Ma. Montelibano* + + VI. Hope In Europe, *Tony Meloto* + + VII. Wealth in Canada, *Tony Meloto* + + VIII. Parenthood: A Sacred Covenant, *Philip S. Chua* + + IX. Are We, Humans, Really Civilize? (Or, are we for the birds.), *Philip S. Chua,* + + X. Save Our Nation, *Philip S. Chua* + + XI. A Time To Pause, *Philip S. Chua* + + XII. The Gawad Kalinga Virus, *Philip S. Chua* + + XIII. A Marching Order For P-Noy,

Violence on Television, *Philip S. Chua* + + 19. Heart to Heart, Attitude Impacts Health, Life, *Philip S. Chua* + + 20. Heart to Heart, Are We Getting Enough Sleep, *Philip S. Chua* + + 21. Heart to Heart, Obesity: A Killer, *Philip S. Chua* + + 22. Are we the disappearing breed of professionals in this country?, *Cesar D. Candari* + + 23. If You Dream It, Do It Retirement, *Cesar D. Candari* + + 24. Only In America, Human Interest Story, *Anonymous*

Writings 11 Book, August, 2011 + + 1. SONA In English and Filipino, *Pres. Benigno Aquino III (P-Noy)* + + 2. Telltale Signs: SONA and the Dogfight Over Spratlys, *Rodel Rodis* + + 3. Why China will not bring the Spratlys issue to the United Nations, *Ted Laguatan* + + 4. Random Thoughts, On Website Demise and On Disunity, *Tatay Jobo Elizes* + + 5. Can Local Private Sector Help Reverse Philippine's Migration Addiction?, *Jeremiah M. Opiniano* + + 6. What Fuels the Passion of Filipinos to Pursue Studies and Work in UK?, *Ofw Journalism Consortium* + + 7. Our Life in the Philippines, *Bob & Carol Hammerslag* + + 8. Reality Check: the Philippines – A Tropical Paradise for the Retiree?, *by Bob & Carol Hammerslag* + + 9. Filipinos Dominate Cruise Ships, *Roger P. Olivares* + + 10. Vargas: Hero, Villain, Tragic Figure?, *Roger P. Olivares* + + 11. Is it Hell to go Back Home?, *Roger P. Olivares* + + 12. The Filipino, now a commodity!, *Roger P. Olivares* + + 13. How US Can Create Jobs, *Rob Ceralvo* + + 14. Modus Operandi - Common Crimes (In Metro Manila, Philippines), *Anonymous* + + 15. Poem, Kabuhayang Bansa At Wika, *Irineo P. Goce (aka KaPule 2 and Leonidas Agbayani)* + + 16. Random Sayings & Advices, *Anonymous*

Writings 12 Book, April 2012 + + 1. Twenty Excuses Filipinos Use, *Orion Perez Dumdum* + + 2. One By One, The Petals Drop, *Julia C. Lagoc* + + 3. Religion & the Scientist, *Honorio M. Cruz, MD* + + 4. The Tales of the Aswang & Bangungot, *Honorio M. Cruz, MD* + + 5. Sex & Politics, *Honrio M. Cruz, MD* + + 6. Autopsy, *Ben Gonzales, MD* + + 7. Geekmocracy, *Mar-Vic Cagurangan* + + 8. Flights: Voice from the Future that Lives in the Past, *Mar-Vic Cagurangan* + + 9. Kaya Natin! Sanctuary, *Marisa Lerias* + + 10. The Days of Courage, *Gerry Partido* + + 11. Earth Day and the Tragedy of a Famous River, *Cesar D. Candari, MD, FCAP Emeritus* + + 12. Few Filipino-American Nonprofits Getting Political, *Erwin De Leon* + + 13. Filipino-American Political Invisibility And Community Organizations, *Erwin De Leon* I+ + 14. I'm 32 and I am still a Virgin, *Jovelyn Bayubay Revilla* + + 15. Hiding Ill-Gotten Wealth, *Jobo Elizes*

Solo Authored Books: + + +

Book A, **Turning Points - Empty Dreams,** *Job Elizes Sr,1968 (Reissue 2009)* + + +
Book B, **Be Considerate - Behaviour Issues,** *Tatay Jobo Elizes (Jr), 2009* + + +
Book C, **Piglets Unlimited - Wealth Untapped,** *Tatay Jobo Elizes, 2009* + + +
Book D, **Out of the Misty Sea We Must,** *Cesar Lumba, 2010* + + +
Book E, **Fulfilled** - *Gonzales Reynaldo, Editor, 2010* + + +

Dook F - **Reflections** - *Bert Guiang, 2010* + + +
Book G, **Writings 7 - My Vintage Pics,** *Tatay Jobo Elizes, 2010* + + +
Book H, **May Bagwis Ang Pag-ibig,** *Percival C. Cruz* + + +
Book I, **Letters To Matrimony,** *Irineo Perez Coce, Ka Pule2, 2011* + + +
Book J, **Songs I Wish You Knew,** *Soledad R. Juan, 2011* + + +

Book K, **Make My Day,** *Larry Henares Jr., 1993, Re-issue 2011* + + +
Book L, **Our Guerrero Family,** *Tatay Jobo Elizes, 2010* + + +
Book M, **Joketor 1,** *Tatay Jobo Elizes, 2011* + + +
Book N, **FaveArt 1,** *Tatay Jobo Elizes, 2011* + + +
Book O, **Beyond idle thoughts,** *MLMunoz, Sept,2011* + + +

Book P, **Cracks In The Armor,** *Mariano Ngan, Oct 2011* + + +
*Book Q, **FaveArt 2,** Tatay Jobo Elizes, 2011* + + +
Book R, **Balitang Kutsero,** *Perry Diaz, Jan 2012* + + +
Book S, **FaveArt3,** *Tatay Jobo, 2011* + + +
Book T, **FaveArt4** *,2012, Tatay Jobo* + + +

Book U, **Stack Family Journals,** *Phil & Fe Stack, 2012* + + +
Book V, **Emily, An Adoption Journey,** *Romerl Elizes, 2012* + + +
Book W, **Hermes Alegre Art Gallery,** *TJ & Hermes, 2012* + + +
Book X, **Masaya Din, Malungkot Din,** *Jovelyn Bayubay Revilla, 2012* + + +

Book Y, **Tiis, Sipag At Tiyaga,** *Raquel Delfin Padilla, 2012* + + +
Book Z, **Until I Meet You,** *Jhackie Eslit Bayobay, 2012* + + +
Book AA, **Buhay At Pag-ibig,** *Argel Lucero Tamayo, 2012* + + +
Book AB, **Hail to the Second Best,** *Dr. Philip Stack, 2012* + + +

Book AC, **Life Bus,** *Mommy Joyce Pineda-Faulmino, 2012* + + +
Book AD, **My Candid Musings,** *Monette Dioquino Calugay, 2012* + + +

Please buy online or give a gift as paperback or kindle edition. All authors and titles are easy to search, trace or find online. Thanks. Self--Publisher Tatay Jobo Elizes

www.ingramcontent.com/pod-product-compliance
Lightning Source LLC
Chambersburg PA
CBHW072317290526
45794CB00002B/694